get better *at* getting better

ADVANCE PRAISE FOR THE BOOK

'Mouli provides a thought-provoking, insightful construct on a topic that I have seen him continuously address over his career. Lucid, practical and logical, this book is a great guide on getting better, every day'—Bharat Puri, managing director, Pidilite Industries

'I have heard of Kaizen and continuous improvement for machines and processes and always wondered why there was no Kaizen process for human beings. This book is the answer to that. Mouli gives you the tools and techniques you require to accelerate your get-better journey. If you want to succeed, stop thinking about success and start thinking about getting better'—Harsh Mariwala, chairman, Marico Ltd

'You don't grow in an organization by just delivering results. You need to continuously get better. Mouli's book makes you realize that and gives you the strategies to get better. Read this book to get an interesting perspective on personal growth'—Piyush Pandey, global chief creative officer, Ogilvy and Mather

'Everyone wants to get ahead; a few want to get better. The ones who get better always get ahead. Mouli's book tells us how all of us can get better'—Shiv Shivakumar, group executive president, corporate strategy and business development, Aditya Birla Group

'Mouli's book shines the light on a critical difference that separates those who succeed—their ability to constantly get better. Far too often we focus on extraneous labels of success, rather than going to the core issue of continuously improving ourselves, which leads to success. I encourage readers to not just read this book but also internalize the concept and apply it consciously. *Get Better at Getting Better* has the potential to change you for good—and make you the best that you can be'—Anand Kripalu, MD and CEO, Diageo India, and member, Diageo Global Executive

'During my long corporate career, I have seen success and failure around me. There is no magical formula, but there can be experiential insights. Understanding and providing a distilled method to success is like a compass. It is very useful to have, so get hold of a compass—like this book'—R. Gopalakrishnan, author and corporate adviser

'Mouli's latest book, *Get Better at Getting Better*, is an ideal sequel to *Catalyst* which gave readers an excellent overview on how to plan a corporate career and how to make it big in the second half by preparing for it in the first half. This book delves into the complex subject of how and why some people succeed more than others despite putting in the same effort. The book, besides being invaluable for corporate careers, will also be extremely useful to HR managers whose job he describes succinctly as "helping people succeed"'—Sam Balsara, chairman, Madison World

'In my years as a consultant at Bain & Company and now with the Godrej Group, my observations resonate with Mouli's powerful insights and conclusions. The most successful people are those who are able to continuously improve themselves and get better. In this book, Mouli lays out a powerful approach for kick-starting your "get-better" journey. A must-read'—Vivek Gambhir, managing director and CEO, Godrej Consumer Products Limited

'I want to congratulate Mouli for producing yet another insightful book on personal development for future leaders who are seeking sustainable success in their careers. I love Mouli's approach of building a simple yet powerful model for getting better in life through a systematic inquiry. Effort is not the only means to your success but need to be supported by a Get-Better Model. I recommend this to all those who are in the early stage of their careers as this book may inspire you to get to the next stage of the success ladder and potentially prevent career derailers'—Annaswamy Vaidheesh, vice president, South Asia, and managing director, GlaxoSmithKline Pharmaceuticals India Ltd

get better *at* getting better

CHANDRAMOULI VENKATESAN

PENGUIN
BUSINESS

An imprint of Penguin Random House

PENGUIN BUSINESS

USA | Canada | UK | Ireland | Australia
New Zealand | India | South Africa | China | Singapore

Portfolio is part of the Penguin Random House group of companies
whose addresses can be found at global.penguinrandomhouse.com

Published by Penguin Random House India Pvt. Ltd
4th Floor, Capital Tower 1, MG Road,
Gurugram 122 002, Haryana, India

Penguin
Random House
India

First published in Portfolio by Penguin Random House India 2019
This edition published in Penguin Business by Penguin Random House India 2024

10 9 8 7 6 5 4 3 2

ISBN 9780670092161

Typeset in Aldine401 BT by Manipal Digital Systems, Manipal
Printed at Replika Press Pvt. Ltd, India

www.penguin.co.in

To Asian Paints, Onida, Cadbury/Mondelez, Pidilite and all the people in those companies who helped me get better.

And to the readers of Catalyst for believing in me.

Contents

1. Introduction 1
2. Get Better at Getting Better 8
3. The Architecture of Getting Better 20

SECTION 1

4. Reviews—It Is Not about the Answer 39
5. Reflection—Improving the Core Capabilities 48
6. The Pilot's View 58

SECTION 2

7. Leveraging Others in Your Organization 72
8. Learning by the Book 83

SECTION 3

9. Making Your Team Better 99
10. Leveraging the External Ecosystem 112

SECTION 4

11. Stagnating Careers and the MBA versus non-MBA Conundrum 126
12. Managing Career Life Cycles 141
13. Getting Better at Meetings 158
14. Start-Ups, Professionals and Education 169

SECTION 5

15. Self-Evaluation 189
16. Making a Get-Better Plan 203
17. Bringing It Together 216

Acknowledgements 233

1

Introduction

I have spent the bulk of my twenty-eight-year career in sales and marketing. However, for three years in the middle, I performed a cross-functional role as the head of HR for what was then Cadbury India Ltd (now Mondelez). In that role, it was important for me to define the purpose of HR for myself, and I defined it as 'helping people succeed'. Each function does something to help the overall business succeed—marketing helps the business succeed through great branding and innovation, while procurement helps by getting the necessary material at the lowest cost and at the highest quality. When I thought about how HR helps the business succeed, it was obvious to me—HR helps by making the people who work in the business succeed. If a lot of people in a company succeed, then the company will automatically succeed, hence my definition of the HR role as 'helping people succeed'. However, this threw up the question 'What makes people succeed?' Why do some people succeed, while others find it very difficult? Why do some people, who are doing moderately well, suddenly hit their take-off point and become wildly successful? Why do some people get stuck and make no progress at all, no matter how hard they try? These are difficult questions to answer. Why and how people succeed is a complex topic with no clear answers and the quest to understand that topic has possessed me for many years now.

The quest to understand this topic led me to write my first book, *Catalyst*. The book was considered very successful and most readers felt like they had started to understand the success model better. The success of the book and the positive feedback, while being very satisfying, also told me that this was a topic people were hungry to get insights into. We are a population that is working very hard to succeed. Sometimes, it is frustrating to us that there are no clear models and frameworks that can direct our efforts more productively. Hence, while I knew that with *Catalyst* I had made a very meaningful start in trying to provide a perspective into that space, there was still a long way to go. I knew the onion had to be unpeeled further, questions explored to greater depths and newer insights required, to illuminate this space to a greater degree. It is to this summit that my journey continues with *Get Better at Getting Better*; I hope it will continue beyond that as well.

While we move beyond *Catalyst* with this new book, my model of gaining insights and exploring the territory of success remains the same as the one I had adopted for my first book—self-awareness, analysing myself and observing others. I tried to understand my own life and career better—why was I successful at some points and less so at others. I observed others keenly, trying to understand why some people succeeded, what drove them and what they did or possessed that was different from others. The success of *Catalyst* also resulted in many people having conversations with me on this topic and helping me understand the questions and issues they were grappling with. The oft-repeated refrain was, 'I am trying hard, putting in all the effort I can, but I am not succeeding'. Explaining the lack of success when people slack off and don't work hard is easy, but life feels unfair when you put in the work but don't get the success that effort deserves. I was quite keen to try to help these people, as well as assist the already successful in accelerating their growth.

Beginning with self-analysis, let me describe my career briefly. I studied engineering at Anna University, Chennai and then did my MBA from XLRI, Jamshedpur, in 1991. I worked for close to a decade in Asian Paints, one year in GE Countrywide, four years in Onida (Mirc Electronics), eleven years in Cadbury/Kraft/Mondelez and have now been working for about two years in Pidilite. If I were to split my journey into different tenures based on how successful I felt, I would possibly say that the first 7–8 years in Cadbury/Kraft/Mondelez were my greatest years and the year in GE Countrywide my lowest. Looking beyond those, I would say I was fairly successful in Asian Paints, successful but to a lesser degree in Onida and I am now on my way to making a positive difference to Pidilite, something I feel confident I can do. Within

Cadbury, I went from strategy to HR to marketing to sales to general management, and I felt I handled all those roles comfortably. The ease with which I traversed the varied requirements of those different roles surprised not only me but others too. As I analysed all this, I realized that in my early career at Asian Paints, I had had a success model, but that success model lacked scalability as it failed when tested under more trying circumstances in GE. By the time I joined Cadbury, I had developed a success model using which I was confident that I could do anything, anywhere, and that confidence continues today. So I believe I have a success model that is scalable. The question is, when did I develop that model, why did I develop it and how could I understand, decode and explain that model to others?

Armed with this understanding, when I observed the careers of others, I could see a pattern emerging. In successful people's careers, there seemed to be a distinct take-off point, after which they were successful in everything they did. There were others who did not experience that take-off point. It was not that they did not taxi or could not make it to the runway, so to speak, but without the take-off, they ended up with only low to moderate success over time.

As I analysed the following:

1. My own feeling that I could succeed in varied situations and environments, and
2. The take-off dynamic in others' careers,

I could sense that there was something common between the two, but it was not apparent at first.

I then started scribbling thoughts, at a very basic level, on which qualities make a person successful in their career. I arrived at the following four areas, which I call 'core capabilities':

1. People skills/relationships/leadership/personal value system
2. Analytical skills/comfort with numbers/logical reasoning
3. Conceptualization and intuitive skills/creativity/insightfulness
4. Organized/disciplined/planned/efficient

Apart from these four areas of capability, there are, of course, the hygiene requirements of hard work and hunger for success, which I am taking as a given in most people.

At first, it seemed to me that there was no clear pattern indicating which among the four core capabilities was more important. Some people were successful because of exceptional analytical skills and decent people skills, while others succeeded based on their conceptualization and creative skills. I finally discovered what seemed to me the breakthrough insight, one common thing I saw with all successful people—the elusive pattern. I observed that they were all excellent at continuously improving the above-mentioned four capabilities in themselves. The differentiating factor was that they had a model based on which they could improve in themselves anything and everything they wanted.

This also explains why I feel confident about my own ability to go into any new situation and succeed. That confidence is not based on already knowing what to do in a new situation, but, instead, on knowing that I have a model that makes me capable of learning and improving what is required to find the answers.

The simple insight into success that this book is based on is that 'success is not about how good you are; it is about how powerful and effective a *model* you have to *improve how good you are*'. I call this model the Get-Better Model (GBM). This book is about delving deeper into this insight, understanding it and then trying to apply it to help you create such a model.

This insight is particularly valuable in today's VUCA (volatile, uncertain, complex and ambiguous) world, where there is continuous change, which needs newer skills and capabilities. The response of people often is to think about continuous re-skilling. Somebody says Artificial Intelligence is the future, so let me enrol in an AI course. Somebody thinks sustainability and pollution control are the future, so let me learn that. That is a good approach, and I do think we must continuously learn new things as the world around us changes. But I also think that can be exhausting—it is quite challenging to predict exactly what will be relevant in the future and learn that in advance. I prefer the simpler approach of developing a model so that when I get to the future, my GBM is capable of learning and adapting to what is required at that time.

In a simple way, this is saying that more than acquiring just the content and the knowledge to succeed, it is important to build the capability to succeed. This book will focus on developing the capability to succeed and then continuously improving that capability.

My first book, *Catalyst*, was about what to do to be successful, while this book is about building the capability, the model to be successful. I would suggest that people who have not yet read *Catalyst* try and read it after reading this book as the two frameworks for success complement each other. For those who have already read my first book, it might be a good refresher to skim through it again after finishing this book. Success is a complex topic and the more often you think about it, the deeper you dive—the more it will help improve your understanding of your success model.

I do have a disclaimer at the start of the book. How to succeed is a very complex topic and there are many ways of getting there. What I am stating is simply my point of view and only one of the ways of thinking about success. It is quite possible that you have a different model that works better for you; by all means, stay true to that. My book is an insight-based book; it is based on the journey of my career, my life and my observations and is not a research-led or scientifically-validated and proven book. Please view it with that lens and feel free to accept or discard what I say based on what you think works for you.

I have a personal mission to help people succeed. This book is written with that missionary zeal and intent. I do hope reading it will help you succeed and, more importantly, increase your confidence in how successful you can be in the future. Happy reading, and all the best.

2

Get Better at Getting Better

Success is not about how good you are; it is about how powerful and effective a *model* you have to improve how good you are—that model is your Get-Better Model, or GBM. The automatic question that follows is, how easy is it to build that model? I got the answer from golf.

I am a passionate golfer. A fabulous aspect of the game is that amateur golfers can spend a lifetime trying to get better at it. Even if you set out to play for recreation, the game consumes you in no time because it is so difficult and challenging. Players practise, hire coaches and take lessons, watch hours of online content on how to swing the club better, observe the professionals on TV and try to learn from that, and so on. But in the end, I observed that despite all these efforts, most people—including myself—don't really get better. This observation about others', and also my own, efforts set me thinking—is getting better at golf that difficult? *Could it be that getting better is more than just trying? Is it about identifying and implementing the right model of improvement?*

Let's consider youngsters who are fresh to golf. I observe these youngsters taking to the game and mastering it easily—kids of 10–12 years start learning and by the time they are fifteen or so, they are playing the game at a level I can't manage after decades of trying. Why is getting better so easy for these kids, but so difficult for me? The obvious reason is age: they are starting at an age at which learning new skills is easy. Thereafter, it becomes progressively more difficult and can border on the impossible after the mid-thirties. This seems to suggest that if we want to get better at something, we must achieve the desired level of proficiency ideally when we are young.

What about work, then?

We start work only in our mid-twenties, when we are already past the most effective learning phase of our life. And we have to sustain that get-better journey late into our lives, usually till our sixties. Building a model to getting better at work is crucial for you and me, but we begin that endeavour at an age when we are possibly past our best learning phase. The implication of this troubled me greatly. Did this mean we cannot easily get better at work, much like me at my golf?

The first and most obvious conclusion I reached was that yes, indeed, the best learning happens at a younger age, and it is difficult to get better at the same pace as one ages. Compare a high-achieving sportsperson who started young with a high achiever at work. A high-achieving sportsperson performs at a level of excellence and effortlessness in their sport that very few people can achieve at work. That is because sportspersons start mastering their craft at a very early age, while we start trying to master work at a much later age. Is there anyone who can claim they are as good at their job as Sachin Tendulkar was at cricket or Tiger Woods at golf or Pele at football? A Virat Kohli possibly learnt more about cricket as a teenager, between the ages of fourteen and nineteen, than I have about work in over twenty-five years of effort in my middle age.

Once I reached that conclusion, the next obvious question was 'What does it take to get better at work?' And as I looked around for the answer, I observed that what I saw at golf was what was largely happening at work. People were trying very hard to get better at work and mostly not making much progress.

I looked around workplaces and found that most people were committed to getting better at work. They implicitly understood that success was about continuously improving how good you were. They were trying to learn new tools and techniques, hiring coaches, mining the experiences and advice of friends, managers and mentors, attending training programmes and online tutorials and diligently reading articles in online and offline media. But similar to my disappointing progress in golf, I saw that most people were making limited progress. Efforts at improvement were made, but the results were not proportionate.

The only difference between golf and work was the lack of a reference point at work. In golf, as I laboured to get better, I could measure myself against the fourteen-year-old next to me. I could see the young kid who, just one month ago, was much worse than me, but had made so much progress that I could not hope to catch up in even a few years. However, at work, there are no such ready reference points. Our reference points are all other people like us—people in their twenties, thirties and forties—trying to get better and making limited progress when measured against the effort they make. Because we don't have the reference point of somebody else who is getting better much faster with much less effort, we never realize that our model for getting better at work is broken. *We do not see that it is an inefficient model that takes a lot of effort and produces meagre results compared to the effort invested.*

More effort or a better machine?

At work, I have often had to deal with the problem of getting more output from a certain machine or a production line. The natural and immediate response most of the time is—let us run the machine longer, let us run extra shifts if required, let us put more people on the job, etc. Occasionally, we step back and wonder if there is a way of improving the productivity and the yield of the machine so that even if it runs the same number of hours as it does now, it will produce a higher output. And when we think like that, more often than not, I have observed that we have indeed managed to improve the output of the machine and more importantly, that improvement is often permanent.

As I spent time thinking about that intractable problem—how to increase the pace of getting better at work despite working from our twenties to our sixties—the answer became obvious to me. Even in trying to achieve more success at work, our natural response is to invest more effort and time, much like our natural response to the machine output problem. We do not step back and ask the question 'How can I improve the machine/model that I have in me, and can I improve its ability to achieve more with the same time and same effort?' It was obvious to me that the answer was in focusing on improving the machine itself, in improving our model of getting better. Thus was born *Get Better at Getting Better*.

As this insight came to me, I also noticed how little effort we put into improving the model. Taking the example of learning—I see people working hard to learn, but making no effort to improve their learning model, the pace and the breadth at which they learn. For instance, when somebody wants to learn a new skill, they might pay money to attend a training programme, but they do not think about how good their learning model is. Is that model efficient, or is it inefficient, thus wasting the time and money spent on the training?

If I were to present it as an equation, it would look like this:

Total learning = Effort put into learning x Quality of learning model

There is actually more to gain by trying to improve the learning model, so that we get more out of even the current effort we are making. This is the difference between me and the fourteen-year-old boy at golf; he is at an age when the learning model for golf is very efficient, and hence effort leads to rapid progress. I am at an age when the learning model for golf is quite inefficient and hence, more effort leads to limited or no progress. I should first try and improve my learning model for golf, otherwise I am just wasting time trying to get better. And I have wasted a decade trying to get better at golf without that simple understanding. My purpose with this book is to ensure that you don't waste decades trying to be successful at work without this simple insight—that you need to improve the GBM first. That is what will provide spectacular results. Hence:

Success = Effort x GBM

The definition of GBM here is 'your model to continuously improve how good you are'. We have often heard of Kaizen/Continuous improvement as a methodology for machines and processes. This book, in a way, is about Kaizen/Continuous improvement for working professionals and human beings.

The question is, what should our approach be for getting better? The keyword for me is *deliberateness*. At a young age, we don't have to go out of our way to get better—we just spend some time doing things and we automatically get better. There is a more natural GBM at a younger age. To get better at golf, all a young kid has to do is play more golf, and the natural GBM will kick in. However, at an older age, just playing more does not make you better. One has to separate playing more and getting better into two different activities. *And getting better has to be a deliberate strategy, independent of just playing more.*

Let me give you an analogy to explain this better. Imagine there is a professional chef who is cooking at a fancy restaurant and there are people like us cooking at home, making routine meals. Who do you think is getting better faster as a cook, and why? I would argue that the chef is getting better faster because there is a lot more deliberateness in a chef's cooking, while daily home cooking is a lot less deliberate and a lot more mechanical. A chef will make a dish, get feedback, tweak the recipe and make a deliberate effort to improve the dish. I want you to reflect on whom you are like at work—like the chef, or like the people who cook mechanically every day and assume they must be getting better in some way by doing that?

You must have a deliberate strategy for getting better, which is different from just working harder. And people who put more deliberate effort into getting better will succeed more than those who simply work harder, as explained in the following pages.

Why is getting better crucial to success?

There are two important factors of success—first, the results you produce here and now, and second, your ability to produce results in the future. Let us take a situation in which there is a job opportunity at a higher level. There are two candidates within the company; both have produced results of the same quality in their previous roles. However, one of the candidates has got much better while producing those results, while the second has not necessarily shown the same progression. Organizations, more often than not, prefer the first kind of candidate, who they think has improved, because they believe that this person has a higher chance of producing results in the next, higher order, more complex role. This can be very frustrating for the second kind of candidate who thinks, 'I produced the same result, so why am I not getting the promotion and the opportunity?'

Producing results is your ticket to continuing at your current level. Producing results is also required for getting a promotion to the next level or finding a more attractive job. However, it is just a hygiene condition—it is *necessary*, not *sufficient*, to get to the higher level. To get to the next level, it is also important to have a GBM that can develop in you the ability to produce results at that next level. Having produced results at the previous level does not guarantee that.

Let's take a sporting analogy to understand that. Most sportspersons have to play at the state level before they can make it to the national team. Hundreds and thousands of players play and produce results at the state level, but only a handful makes it to the Indian team. That is because the selectors who choose the national team know that producing results at the state level is no guarantee that those players will produce results at the national level.

They are asking the crucial question—has this person got so much better at the state level that they can succeed at international tournaments? Can this person handle the pressure of international competition? The answer to these questions lies in the quality of the GBM the player has developed playing for their state. There are many instances in Indian cricket of players who were phenomenally successful at the Ranji trophy competition for inter-state cricket, but failed at the international level.

The exact same principle applies in the corporate and business world too. If you produce results only at the current level without getting better while doing so, your ability to produce results in the future is compromised and you are unlikely to succeed at higher level roles.

It is a great challenge for most people to separate producing results and getting better and see them as two different things. And that often results in us giving inadequate priority to getting better.

Prioritize getting better

There is a natural tendency among us to prioritize generating results for ourselves and for our organizations. We do not put a priority on getting better while generating those results, thinking incorrectly that if we produce results, we must be automatically getting better.

At work, the responsibility for each one of us getting better rests squarely on our own shoulders. However, we don't put enough emphasis on it. The most visible symptom of this is the loyal, committed employees at the mid-level of organizations who, with tremendous passion and commitment, produce results for many years without any focus on getting better for future career success. Such people stagnate in their careers despite producing results and, in organizational parlance, are often referred to as loyal soldiers who will keep fighting the battle, but will never become generals. We have all seen them—somebody who has been a zonal manager in the same zone for many years, somebody in a factory who has been doing the same role for many years, somebody in accounts who has been discharging the same duties for many years, etc. These loyal soldiers focus on producing more results for the next year without understanding that if they don't change their priority from getting results to getting better, there will be no career progress for them.

Results are transitory and belong not only to us but also to our teams and the company. But the extent to which you have got better in producing that result is not transitory; it is permanent and belongs solely to you. It is not a badge of loyalty to say, 'I focus on results for my company over my own progress.' We must be committed and loyal to the company we work in —I have always believed that and practised it—but not by sacrificing our future success. And truly evolved companies encourage us to keep getting better while producing results.

Having said the above, I don't want to convey the impression that producing results and getting better are contradictory to each other. I think there is a lot in common between the two and we must not see them as either-or. At the same time, we must recognize they are not the same either. We have to manage our careers towards two outcomes. The organization and our bosses will drive the push for results; the prioritization of getting better has to be driven by us.

We have all heard 'You are in charge of your own development' from HR at various times. Our response is often cynical, thinking HR is making an excuse so that they don't have to invest in our development. Without seeking to defend HR, it is important to recognize that that is the truth. Only we ourselves are responsible for our own improvement, nobody else is. HR can be a facilitator, your boss can help, but the final accountability is yours and yours alone. So please, prioritize getting better, and being deliberate is the key to that.

Get-better summary

1. Success is not about how good you are, but about how powerful and effective a *model* you have to *improve how good you are*.
2. Success = Effort x GBM
3. The GBM at work is difficult to develop since we start on it at an age when it is not the easiest thing to do and we have to sustain that development till the very late age of almost sixty years.
4. Most people have a poor/average GBM and instead of trying to improve the model, they just put more effort into being successful. The greater focus should be to improve the effectiveness of the model you have, and deliberateness is the key to that.

5. Just producing results is not enough for success—while producing results, you have to get better so as to improve your ability to produce results in the future. Hence, it is important for us to prioritize getting better.

3

The Architecture of Getting Better

The *purpose* of getting better is being able to respond better to the future; if we get better, our response to the future will be better than our response today to similar situations. If we don't, it becomes difficult to succeed.

An important question is to determine *what* areas you have to get better in and *how* you get better in those areas. Let us say you are trying to get healthier. What would you assess at the end of a few months to know if you are indeed getting healthier? In all probability you would assess your weight and possibly if you get tired easily, etc. You know you have become healthier if your weight has reduced and you don't get tired easily. To be able to achieve this you have to exercise regularly and have a diet plan that you follow with discipline. In this analogy 'what' you are trying to get better at is reducing your weight and increasing your stamina and 'how' you are doing that is through regular exercise and diet.

In a similar way, for getting better at work, it is important to understand 'what' areas we are trying to get better at and 'how' will we get better there. That 'what' for work needs you to make progress on two fronts:

1. Don't stop at knowing the answer; get to the method of finding the answer.
2. Build your core capabilities.

When we go through a situation, we learn some answers at the end of it. However, if we stop at knowing the answers and do not go into the method used to find the answers, we will struggle in the future when faced with more complex situations. The simplest example of this is multiplication tables. If somebody asks us what 12 x 12 is and if you immediately say 144 without having to calculate it, that is knowing the answer. If you know the method of multiplication, then that's the method by which you find the answer. Knowing the answers does not work beyond the easy questions, like 3 x 3 or 12 x 12. If somebody asks us what 734 x 498 is, we won't know the answer. We have to use the method of finding the answer, which is multiplication. The exact same thing happens at work—there are many answers we know and remember by virtue of precedent, or because somebody taught us. But we often stop at knowing the answers, we do not master the method of finding the answers and hence struggle when faced with more complex situations.

The second area of getting better is building your core capabilities. Let's take the example of a person who has poor listening skills and hence does not understand the problem accurately to begin with. Unless this person fixes their ability to listen, knowing the method of finding the answers might not help as the problem for which the answer is to be found will not be clear. The core capabilities are in four areas, as defined in chapter 1:

1. People skills/relationships/leadership/personal value system
2. Analytical skills/comfort with numbers/logical reasoning/rigour
3. Conceptualization and intuitive skills/creativity/insightfulness
4. Organized/disciplined/planned/efficient

If you have to assess if you have got better in the last one year then check if these two things have improved. Your method of finding the answers should have improved for both existing situations as well as new situations. The same should be the case with your core capabilities. If these two things have changed positively, you have got better; if not, you have not got better, however hard you worked in that one year.

The 'how' to get better is what I call the Get-Better Model (GBM), your *model to continuously get better.* If you have a good GBM, it means you can get better at a rapid rate. For a given amount of work, a superior GBM will get you to knowing more methods of finding answers and better capabilities.

A GBM is made up of four key components and these must be practised deliberately for getting better:

1. *Getting better by yourself:* This is about deliberately getting better from what you do on a daily basis by yourself, without external help.
2. *Getting better by leveraging others*: This is about deliberately leveraging all external resources available to you to get better.
3. *Make others get better*: This is about deliberately building an ecosystem around you that multiplies your efforts.
4. *Making and implementing a get-better plan*: This is about deliberately making a plan and implementing it to get better in a few areas of focus.

The four components of the GBM constitute the 'how' to get better and each will be independent sections of the book. I have briefly given an outline of each in the following paragraphs.

Section 1: Getting better by yourself

There are two ways of thinking about getting better. One is to say that I will take other people's help and undertake specific efforts, like a training programme. This is the conventional teaching method—a teacher helps you get better. The second is to say that whatever I am doing on a daily basis must make me better—that is where getting better by yourself comes in. If everything we do every day, every hour, makes us better, we have a truly excellent GBM that will bring us great success. For that, you must be able to get better by yourself without any external help. This section will cover the tools and techniques we can practise to improve the rate at which we get better by ourselves.

Section 2: Getting better by leveraging others

To understand the concept of leveraging others to get better, let us take a sports analogy. All sports teams have support staff consisting of coaches, physiotherapists, psychologists, statisticians, etc. What is the purpose of this support staff? They don't play the game, they don't win games; then why does such a large army of people accompany a sports team? They are there for one sole purpose, which is to help the players get better. A sports team whose players keep getting better with every match will win more games—that is the purpose of the coaching staff.

It is the same in companies and organizations, our workplaces. There are coaches, statisticians, videographers, psychologists, etc. in companies, only they are not labelled that way, and more importantly, it is not conveyed clearly to others that one of their most important objectives is to continuously make people better. As a player in a sports team, you know clearly that the support staff is available for your betterment, but as a player (employee) in a company, you don't realize that there are many resources available to help you get better continuously. We think that the quest for improvement and greater success is a solo effort. This section will cover techniques that will help you exploit all the external resources available to you.

Section 3: Make others better, build the ecosystem

None of us becomes successful or produces results based on only what we do. There are a set of people who support us in producing results. For example, if you are a film director, the cameraperson and the music director are crucial parts of the ecosystem. However good the film director is, a good film cannot be made with poor photography and music. Hence, when the director thinks about getting better, should the thought be only 'how can I become better', or should the thought be 'how can I make my ecosystem better too?' If we go back to the why of the GBM, it is because we want to produce better results for the same effort. Enhancing our ecosystem will get us better results for the same efforts we make.

The key components in our ecosystem are our team, our vendors and our partners. I have seen many successful people who, by themselves, were not the best, but worked actively towards assembling and cultivating a high-quality ecosystem. I have seen that these people have succeeded more than others, who, on an individual basis, were better, but did not assemble and cultivate a superior ecosystem. How to make that ecosystem better will be the third section of this book.

Section 4: Application of get-better principles

While the first three sections cover the overall get-better tools and techniques, this section will cover some specific applications of those tools and techniques.

A specific chapter in this section will be devoted to those who, despite making great effort and achieving decent results, experience career stagnation. Unknown to them, the core issue is that they have stopped getting better. They have to find out how to unlock their GBM based on the principles given in this book and reignite their career. Please read through to the end of the book to reach that chapter, do not jump to it directly, because if you don't pick up the other concepts on the way, you won't be able to solve the problem by just reading that chapter.

There is also a chapter on how the get-better principles work in different contexts, like start-ups. Sometimes, it is assumed that these principles work only for people in conventional jobs in conventional organizations. That is not correct—they apply to start-ups and to professionals like doctors, lawyers, etc.

Important applications of the get-better principles are in managing meetings and managing career life cycles—these are standalone chapters in this section. Most of us lament about the time wasted in meetings and its non-productive nature. This section will help you get better at meetings. It will also show you how you can get better at managing career life cycles and be equally effective in all stages of a career life cycle.

Section 5: Make and implement a get-better plan

There are many things we can get better at, and it is not possible to simultaneously get better at everything at the same time. This section will cover how to make a get-better plan to identify which areas you want to improve yourself in and which techniques you should use to go about it. This section will also provide ways of implementing that plan in a disciplined way. A key part of improving anything is to know where you stand. This section will give you self-evaluation tools to determine how good your current GBM is and how much progress you have made.

Hence, if one were to look at a thumbnail sketch to getting better, it would be:

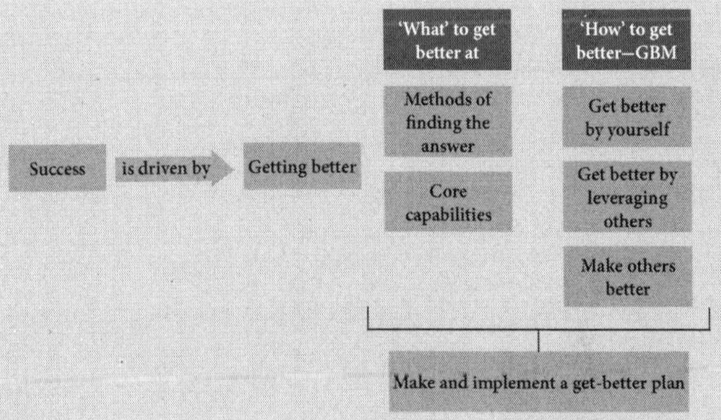

Success is not about how good you are, but about how good a model you have to improve how good you are; it is about how much better you are getting. 'What' you have to become better in is getting more/better methods of finding the answer and improving your core capabilities. The 'how' of getting better is by building the GBM which has four components: getting better by yourself, getting better by leveraging others and making others better; the fourth component, making a get-better plan and implementing it, integrates the 'what' and the 'how' in a continuous improvement cycle. A good GBM will result in you getting better rapidly and make you highly successful at work.

I also have some thoughts on the best way to use this book. Firstly, I do recommend that you read it more than once—the processing and internalizing of concepts is much better that way. This is not a storybook, but a book that will help you succeed. Spending an additional 6–8 hours to read it a second time might be a good investment to consider making for your success. There are also many places in the book where I will request you to put the book down and do an exercise or think about something. Please don't ignore those and keep moving ahead, as that will reduce what you can get out of this book. Lastly, to get great value from the book, my one tip is that you read the book and then try to help somebody else practise the concepts in it. When you try to talk about these concepts to others, your own understanding and conviction will be significantly strengthened and you will feel much more confident in the application of these concepts to yourself. Welcome to *Get Better at Getting Better*—it is a lifelong journey.

Get-better summary

1. The purpose of getting better is to be able to respond to the future better. If our response to a situation in the future is not significantly better than our response in the present, we will not be successful.
2. The first question is being clear about 'what' to get better at. There are two aspects to it:
    a. Don't stop at knowing the answer; get to the method of finding the answer.
    b. Build your core capabilities.

3. 'How' to get better is by developing a strong GBM, *the model to continuously get better.*
4. Your GBM has four key components, which you should practise in a deliberate way to get better rapidly:
   a. Get better by yourself.
   b. Get better by leveraging others.
   c. Make others better.
   d. Make and implement a get-better plan.

SECTION 1

Get better by yourself

Let us take the analogy of a sportsperson trying to improve their skills. They play many matches and then take a break. In that break, they analyse mistakes, take coaching support and try and use that support to improve their game. It is an absolutely legitimate way to get better.

Now consider another sportsperson who, even when in the middle of a match, is able to assess what they are doing right and where they are falling short, and is able to make some immediate adjustments for a better performance. This is how the best sportspersons seem to play. A good batsman or batswoman will face a few balls and quickly understand the opposing team's strengths and the playing conditions. They are then able to activate their model to get better at facing the next ball. This person can get better by themselves without a coach and without having to take a break.

In simple words, these are two different ways of getting better. One is to use external assistance, like training programmes and coaches, identifying specific times to get better, taking breaks from day-to-day work and focusing on getting better. This method works on the assumption that day-to-day work and getting better are two different things and need to be done at different times. Hence, to get better, I need help from others and I have to allocate dedicated time and space to it, separate from what I do every day. The entire training and coaching model is built on this premise.

The second way is to infuse into your model the skill of getting better by yourself using the day-to-day work. Instead of waiting for a practice session or a training programme, we can deliberately leverage what we do every day to get better continuously. This is what I call 'get better by yourself' and sometimes even 'get better every hour'.

I am certainly not saying that get better sessions like training programmes, coaching, etc., or the help of others, are not required. However, those alone are not enough. I have found that the single most important cause of success is our ability to learn from what we do every day and that is possible only if you equip yourself to get better.

I believe that getting better every day by yourself is more important than the specific efforts you take once in a while for the following reasons:

1. The bulk of our time goes into our daily and hourly activities. The typical workplace is different from the sports context, where there are many days or weeks available between games to undertake efforts at improvement. At our workplaces, the time available for breaks is limited. Hence, an approach in which we do not productively utilize every hour, every day to get better, and wait for the specific breaks instead, is unlikely to work.

2. Waiting for specific periods and not focusing on getting better on a daily basis also means that the benefit of getting better will not be visible in the results here and now. If we focus on getting better this hour, this day, it could have a beneficial impact on our results right from tomorrow, as opposed to waiting for a break later for getting better.

Since getting better every hour, every day is important, it requires us to build a GBM capable of doing that. And that GBM has to enable you to get better by yourself; it is not possible to hire a coach or attend a training session every day.

Getting better by yourself every hour, every day might seem very challenging and intimidating. It might feel like it will take too much effort, focus and concentration. You might feel it is idealistic, impractical. I don't think so—once you build the habit, once you build the discipline, it will be quite easy.

Start by wanting to get better every hour

The starting point to getting better by yourself lies in intent and objective setting. Currently, most of us walk out each morning thinking, 'I must produce results today, I must be effective and productive today,' but seldom do we set out in the morning thinking, 'I must get better today, I must get better every hour.' This lack of intent is at the heart of poor GBMs. We simply do not have those expectations from ourselves or prioritize the need to get better every hour, every day.

Let me try and explain the impact of intent and objective setting using an exercise as an example. Let us say that today, Shailaja has an important meeting, the annual budget meeting. Like most of us, she goes into the meeting with the objective of getting her proposed budget approved with minimal changes. She has a very clear *results* objective—the approval of her budget. What would happen if instead of a results objective, she went into the meeting with a *get-better* objective? It could be, 'I want to get better at having good budget conversations and at getting my budget approved.' Let us assume that happens and she changes the objective of her meeting from a *results* objective to a *get-better* objective. Try and reflect on the following questions:

1. Will Shailaja's results be compromised if she goes in with a get-better objective as opposed to a results objective?
2. Will the extent to which she gets better be the same or different in the two situations?

In my experience, I would say, when you change the intent from a results-first intent to a get-better intent, the result is seldom adversely impacted. In some cases, the result might actually improve. However, the dramatic change is the extent to which we get better. It changes how we prepare for the meeting, how we engage in the conversation and how we review ourselves after the conversation. Those have a great impact on making us better and on how we approach the next budget meeting.

Having the intent and expecting ourselves to get better, every hour, every day, is the foundation of getting better. And the key to that is to not only have *results* objectives but also have *get-better* objectives for important days and activities. So the next time you go into an important meeting, set yourself the objective of how to get better at engaging and managing in that meeting; the next time you are hiring for a job in your team, set yourself the objective of how to get better at hiring; the next time you are visiting the field or making a customer visit, set yourself the objective of how to get better at customer visits. The moment you start to have these expectations from yourself and have the intent of getting better every hour, every day, you will be amazed at how things change. Put this book down and recollect the most important activities you did last week. Now ask yourself, did you get better adequately for the time spent on them? What would you have done differently if you had a get-better objective instead of a results objective for those activities? Take a few minutes to think about these questions.

Once you have the intent and set the right objectives for getting better every hour, every day, the next important thing is the technique. There are three key techniques explained over the next three chapters:

1. The review process, to take us from knowing the answer to the method of finding the answer.

2. The reflection process, to improve our core capabilities.
3. The pilot's view, to operate from a higher plane than our current one.

Getting better each *hour* by yourself is a dramatic phrase that I use to convey the importance of getting better continuously based on what you do on a day-to-day basis. You mustn't take it literally. Sometimes, people get stressed and anxious, even intimidated, at the thought of having to get better every hour. My intent is that you use daily work to get better, that you use important events to get better, and develop a GBM in which you are continuously improving.

4

Reviews—It Is Not about the Answer

An hour can make a difference to your future. Let me give you an example to explain why I say so. Say three people, Ajay, Vijay and Sanjay, feel hungry well past midnight and decide to go out in search of a restaurant. After spending an hour driving around without directions, they find a place called Shetty's Restaurant and eat there. So here is the situation we have—each of the three has spent one hour of his time, so the input is the same. The question is how much better each one of them has got in that one hour. And since the purpose of getting better is to respond better in the future, we will assess their getting better based on how each one responds in the future.

After that one hour, Ajay says to himself, 'Remember Shetty's Restaurant stays open late at night. So in the future, when you get hungry, don't drive around randomly—go straight to Shetty's.' Ajay has got better and can respond to the hunger problem better in the future as long as he is in the same city as Shetty's.

Vijay says to himself, 'Shetty's Restaurant was opposite the railway station. There is a good chance that eating joints opposite the railway station are open at night. Hence, whenever I get hungry late at night, instead of driving around, I will locate the nearest railway station and find a place to eat.' Vijay has got even better than Ajay, and he can address the hunger problem even in a different city, as long as there is a railway station there.

Sanjay says to himself, 'Shetty's Restaurant was opposite the railway station, which means the same thing applies to all transport hubs, like airports and bus terminals. Hence, in the future, when I get hungry in the night, instead of simply driving around, I will locate the nearest transport hub and find something to eat.' Sanjay has improved even more than Vijay, and he can address the hunger problem even in a city that does not have a railway station, as long as there is a transport hub there.

All three have spent one hour in the effort. And all three have got better as a result of that one hour. In the future, when they get hungry in the night, their response will be better than in this instance, when they drove around randomly. However, they have not got better equally. Ajay got marginally better, while Sanjay got significantly better. Was the difference because Sanjay made a greater effort than Ajay? That is not the case. All three put in the same effort—they all drove for one hour. However, for the same effort, Sanjay became much better, which indicates that the difference was in the GBM. Sanjay had a 'get better by himself' model which was superior to Ajay's. Pause for a moment and think about who will be more successful,

Ajay or Sanjay. And think about how effective you are at getting better every hour—are you closer to Ajay's level or Sanjay's? Write down your assessment here:

....

....

....

Most people I see at work get better like Ajay. Their GBM is quite inefficient and hence, despite putting in a lot of effort, they do not get better quickly. Effective review is pivotal to convert the hour you spend into getting better outcomes.

Why do a review?

The problem in this case is finding a restaurant open at night. If you look at the two responses above closely, you will notice that Ajay's improvement stopped at knowing the answer to the problem, whereas Sanjay's improvement was in finding the method that led to the answer, not the answer itself. Shetty's is the answer, locating the nearest transport hub is the method of finding the answer. This is the million-dollar insight—*if you want to get better, you should not stop at just knowing the answer, but get to the method*.

It is important for you to understand the difference between knowing the answer and the method of finding it. Let us assume for a moment that you know the answer to a certain situation and it is the perfect one. The same situation recurs after a few years, but by now, you have forgotten the answer. Will you be able to derive the answer from first principles again? This ability to derive the answer is what I call the method of finding the answer.

An example I gave was in the multiplication of two numbers. Knowing that 3 x 3 = 9 is knowing the answer, but the fact that you know that answer does not mean you are good at multiplication, which is the method of finding the answer. To give a business example, let us take a sales situation in which you have to decide which products/SKUs should be stocked in a certain retail outlet. If you already have a list of SKUs for that store from your boss, that is knowing the answer. But if you do not have a list, your ability to draw up a list based on the other products that store sells, the location of the store, the kind of customers it has, what the neighbouring stores sell, etc. is the method of finding the answer.

Only if you have mastered the method of finding the answer will you be able to respond to future situations. Situations will keep changing, the answers won't remain the same. The answers from the past will cease to be relevant, but your method of finding the answer, once improved, will help you respond better to all future situations.

Typically, when we start our careers, we don't know the answers to most situations. However, that does not mean that the company you work in does not have those answers; most of the answers are already known to the people who work there. For example, your boss. In the first 5–10 years of our careers, we perform mostly those tasks for which somebody has already worked out an answer—this is the way it has always been done, this is how we did it last year and it worked and so on. This way, we end up getting many answers without having to find them ourselves. After the first few years, in which you rely largely on ready answers, you start getting into positions where the requirement is to find answers to new situations, and you start to get tested. Now, suddenly, you move from a career phase where you are winning, thanks to already existing answers, to a phase where you have to win by finding new answers. Many people stumble at this stage.

How does one go from knowing the answers to the method of finding the answers? That is where effective reviews come in. Let us now help Ajay get better by himself. Ajay has stopped at the answer—'Shetty's'. We want him to get to the method of finding the answer.

The means to that is a self-review based on the question 'What could I have done to have got a *better outcome* for the one hour I spent?'

As Ajay reviews himself using that question and tries to answer it, let us go through how his thinking is likely to progress:

1. I did solve the problem of midnight hunger pangs and found an answer; I found Shetty's.
2. The better outcome for me in this situation is not getting the answer; it is about getting to that answer faster and more efficiently.
3. To find it faster, I would have to change the way I looked for it. I drove around randomly. Instead,

I could have developed a hypothesis about where I could find food in the night and drive there directly.

4. A hypothesis could be that food would possibly be available in places where there is a flow of people even in the night, like railway stations, airports, bus terminals, etc.
5. Hence, let me first drive to one of those places and find a place to eat.

By reviewing himself based on the question, 'What could I have done to get to a better outcome in that one hour?' Ajay would have followed the above line of thought and come to the realization that while the answer was Shetty's, the method of finding the answer was locating the nearest transport hub. To get to a better outcome, you have to decode the method of finding the answer. That is why a review based on trying to get to a better outcome actually gets you to the method.

Most of you would think that you are also capable of the same logical thinking and conclusions as Ajay. The simplest and easiest way to get better every hour is to review yourself with the question 'What could I have done to get to a better outcome in this one hour?' It does not require superhuman abilities; you and I can do it. I do want to repeat that the 'hour' is not to be taken literally; it can be a day, an activity, an important meeting—anything of consequence you did using which you want to get better.

I want you to practise this once now. Think of an instance in the last one week when somebody else gave you the answer to a particular situation. You used that answer and got to an outcome in that situation. Now practise the review process—'What could I have done for a better outcome?' Take five minutes doing that. It is important to internalize this process.

Deliberateness to build the habit

The core challenge of getting better is to build the habit and have the discipline of getting to the method, even in situations where you can get the answer easily. If you don't build the *deliberate* habit in easy situations, by the time you are faced with difficult situations, you would not have built the capability to get to the answer. If you don't first learn the method of multiplication in 12 x 12, you cannot learn it when you are faced with 734 x 498.

Building that deliberate habit is the purpose of the 'better outcome' in the review question 'What could I have done for a better outcome?' An alternate review question could have been 'I know the answer, but what is the method of finding the answer'? The reason I prefer the question with 'better outcome' in it is because it is more motivating to do a review where there is a probability of improving the outcome. In the early years of your career, you will get many answers from others. You are not motivated to find the method to the answer when you already have the answer. But if the challenge set is to improve upon the answer that somebody else gives you, then you find it more motivating and, in that process, you end up finding the method also. This will ensure you start to build the habit.

I want to tell you the story of Radhakrishnan, who worked as a young sales manager in Chennai. RK, as he was known, was reporting to Arasu, a veteran of the Chennai market. Arasu gave specific instructions to RK on which suburbs were important, which stores were important, which promotions would work in which stores, how to manage the relationships with different distributors, etc. RK followed those instructions and got fantastic results. As a consequence of those results, RK thought he had become a very good sales manager and requested his company to make him the regional manager in charge of all of south India. One fine day, his company obliged. That was the start of his troubles—when RK got to Bengaluru and had to coach the sales manager there, he was found wanting. He did not know the retailers there, he did not know which promotions would work and so on, and he had limited value to add to the sales manager's work there. Soon his company asked him to leave, because the primary job of a regional manager is to coach the managers reporting to them.

I hope each of you understands the message of this story. We are the Google generation—we type a question and get the answer. We don't bother about how that answer was arrived at. When we start our careers, the bulk of the results we produce is because of our bosses and others who give us the answers. If all you do is implement those answers, you will produce the results, but you are not getting better, you are not learning the method to find the answers yourself. So when you have to lead others, you will struggle. The greatest habit we have to build is that even when we get the answer, we must strive to understand the method. That comes from an attitude that says, 'I want to improve upon the outcome and the answer that I got through the self-review process.'

Sometimes senior people think reviews are only for the juniors, I already have a method of finding the answers, so I don't need to practise reviews as intensely. The crucial thing is to see if these methods are evolving and improving or remaining the same. *If your method of finding the answer has remained the same for that situation for very long, then it is possible that you have stopped getting better and started stagnating*. Push yourself to improve your methods to finding the answer through your review process.

Get-better summary

1. If you want to get better, you should not stop at knowing the answer, but get to the method of finding the answer.
2. To get to the method, we need a very disciplined and effective self-review based on the question 'What could I have done to get a better outcome?'
3. When we are juniors, we get many of the answers from others. Even when we get answers from others, it is important for us to build the habit of getting to the method of finding the answer.
4. As seniors, the purpose of reviews is to continuously *improve* your method of finding the answers to different situations.

5

Reflection—Improving the Core Capabilities

Circling back to Shetty's, in the context of Ajay and Sanjay, we had agreed that

1. Ajay had stopped at the answer 'in the future, when I get hungry, I will go to Shetty's directly', while Sanjay had gone beyond and discerned the method of finding the answer: 'In the future, when I get hungry, I will locate the nearest transport hub'.
2. In the last chapter, I had explained that a review process that is done well is the key to moving from the answer to getting the method of finding the answer.

Let us agree that Ajay implemented the review process and reached the same level as Sanjay in that particular example. The next time Ajay and Sanjay do a different task for one hour each, at the end of that one hour, will both get better to the same extent or will Sanjay again end up ahead? It is possible that Sanjay has an inherently superior model to benefit from each hour and hence the next time too he might end up getting better than Ajay. Each time you do a review, it improves your method to find the answer for the situation you are in. However, if you want to fundamentally improve the capabilities you have, then you have to go beyond review to reflection. *Review is about improving the method to finding the answer in a situation; reflection is about improving your core capabilities such that you can do it in every situation, each time.*

Let me give you an example to help understand this. We have all taken exams at school. After the exam we often discussed with friends if we got all the answers right. It is then that we discovered that we got an answer wrong because of a silly mistake or because we did not read the question properly. Will discovering that mistake prevent silly mistakes like this from happening in the future? Unlikely, as for that the core capability issues that led this to happen in the first place has to be improved. In this case, the core capabilities of concentration and detail orientation. If those capabilities don't improve you will continue to make silly mistakes. The purpose of reflection is to identify and get better in the core capabilities.

I had highlighted the core capabilities required at work in the earlier chapters:

1. People skills/relationships/leadership/personal value system
2. Analytical skills/comfort with numbers/logical reasoning/rigour

3. Conceptualization and intuitive skills/creativity/ insightfulness
4. Organized/disciplined/planned/efficient

Going back to Shetty's example, Ajay performed the review, answering the question, 'What could I have done to get a better outcome in that one hour I spent?' This helped him move from knowing the answer to the method of the answer.

Now Ajay is keen on improving his core capabilities from that situation. For that he has to ask himself, 'Why did I not arrive at that better outcome the first time itself?' That is the reflection question.

If Ajay were to ask the reflection question, there are many answers he could come up with, like the two below:

1. I did not develop any hypothesis up front, I did not take those few initial minutes to think about possible places that would be open even in the night. Instead, I started driving randomly right from the start.
2. I did not have the deductive capability to think that places that are crowded at night might have restaurants. So while I knew railway stations were teeming with people at night, I would not have connected that with the possibility of a restaurant being open around one of them.

You will notice that the answers here have moved to more fundamental capabilities like creative hypothesis generation and analytical-deductive capability. The interesting thing about reflection is that you start to see patterns of the same capability issue in different situations. So if one of Ajay's two problems is that he does not take the time for creative hypothesis generation at the beginning, and if that is a core capability issue for him, it will show up in reflections for multiple tasks over time. And as Ajay reflects and finds that this issue shows up again and again, gradually, he will start to drive a fundamental change in himself. He will start to take some time at the start and generate hypotheses to deliver a superior outcome, and that will slowly but steadily become a core part of how he operates.

Reflection in effect is a hindsight process of understanding your capability issues. After the event is over, you find out for yourself what capability issues prevented you from performing at your best the first time itself.

Review and reflection might sometimes feel like they overlap, but they are actually quite different. To make it abundantly clear, let's summarize the differences below:

	Review	**Reflection**
Purpose	Go from answers to the method of finding the answers	Discover the core capability issues to be improved
Question	What could I have done to arrive at a better outcome?	Why could I not get the better outcome the first time itself?
Answers	Discover the underlying method of finding the answers	Typically start with 'I' and are about core capabilities.
Application	After each day, each activity, each project, etc. Get to the method each time	Look for patterns in the answers over many reflections and tackle the capability issues that come up repeatedly

Reflection is a lot more difficult to do than it seems. When people ask themselves, 'Why did I not get the better outcome in the first place itself?' they often end up with superficial answers that do not go to the root of the problem. You can get better only if you go to the core of the capabilities you need to improve. If your answers are superficial, if your answers tend to externalize the problem to people or factors beyond your control, even a lot of time spent on reflection may not make you better.

In my own life, I have learnt this the hard way in some areas. Through the first 15–17 years of my career, I often got the sense that while I was good at the intellectual aspects and breakthrough thinking, I was not very good at people management and building relationships. I kept ignoring that aspect, externalizing it, and not really trying to get better in that area. Things came to a head when I made a cross-functional move and became the HR head of Cadbury India in 2007. Suddenly, I was in a chair where I was constantly judging how good others in the organization were as people managers and at building relationships. The penny finally dropped. The kind of things that I saw poor people managers doing were things that I had often done before. I had to first get better as a people manager and at building relationships myself before I judged others. And that triggered a change in me that was significant and valuable for me going forward. But it also set me thinking on a set of questions:

1. Why could I not reflect and internalize the problem earlier? Why was it so easy to tell myself that people

management was a minor irritant and not a major problem I had to resolve?

2. If I had not ignored that aspect all these years, if I had got better earlier, would I have achieved even more success?

And that is when I realized the need for much better reflection, much more honest reflection, which leads us to the core issues we need to tackle. Living with a problem for a long time does not mean it does not exist. My strong advice to each of you is that do not ignore that niggling thought at the back of your mind that says you need to get better at something. Bring it to the front of the mind, be brutally honest with yourself and improve in those aspects. You will be much more effective and successful for it. And to help you do this, I have two tips on how to do superior reflection.

Specific reflection

The first method for better reflection is what I call 'specific reflection'. Imagine you have launched a new product. After the launch, you do a review and you find that the supply of the new product was inadequate for the market, in turn causing a business loss. As you analyse, you realize that the cause of that was the incorrect forecast for the new product, which resulted in low supply. So the reflection question, instead of being a generic 'Why could I not get a better outcome for the new product in the first place?' now becomes a more targeted question: 'Why could I not get the forecast for the new product right at the start?' As a response to this question, you might get answers like:

1. I did not put enough analytical rigour in the forecasting process; I did it superficially.
2. I did not engage with and seek the views of all key stakeholders in the forecast and went with my judgement only.
3. I was not insightful enough to catch the changing market trend towards the segment the new product is in.

The specific reflection method ensures that you cannot get away by giving superficial answers to the generic reflection question. It is a much more targeted question and demands specific answers, which then are get-better areas for you. And you may also notice that all the answers here started with 'I did not . . .' Each time you reflect, make sure your answers start with 'I', as opposed to externalizing the problem to others and the environment.

Outside-in reflection

Another good way for superior reflection is the 'outside-in' method of reflection. This is about answering the reflection question as an outsider or as somebody else, not yourself. For example, you could visualize somebody else who often gives you improvement feedback which, while being critical, is right and fair. And then you visualize what that person would say about why you could not get a better outcome in the first place. It is like stepping out of your own shoes and seeing yourself from another's person's eyes. What would that person identify as the reasons, the capability issues, that prevented you from getting the better outcome in the first place?

I once had a colleague who was exceptionally smart but burnt many bridges and was somewhat arrogant. He wasn't self-aware. As a coach, I had often asked him to reflect on this issue, but found that he was always superficial and never internalized this as an area he had to get better at. Then, one day, I sat him down and said, 'Now imagine your father observed you every day at work, saw how you interacted with other people and gave you feedback—what would he say to you? Your father does not know others here; he only knows you. So the entire feedback would be only for you.' And I made him write the feedback he thought his father would give him. That was the first time I saw him internalize the issue of relationships, which he needed to improve on. In this example, I forced the outside-in reflection on him. I would urge you, however, to not wait for somebody to force it on you, but to practise it yourself.

Going to higher quality reflection through either specific reflection or outside-in reflection is particularly important in situations where you are trying hard, but making limited progress. In these situations, what we do often is try even harder, but the real issue is that we lack the insight into why we are not making progress. Which of our core capabilities is holding us back? Unless you solve that, you will not make progress simply by putting in more effort.

A great symptom of superficial reflection is the feeling of being frustrated. When you experience frustration, it is because you think you are doing everything right yet not getting the results and success that you deserve. It is a classic case of externalizing the problem. Frustration often sets off a vicious cycle in careers—the more frustrated you get, the less you focus on getting better and the worse your career gets. When you get frustrated, break out of this vicious, negative spiral by practising high-quality reflection to understand what you should get better in, without externalization, and then focus on that.

Reflection is not about finding weaknesses and mistakes, but about finding areas for improvement. It is not something that somebody else does to criticize you; it is something you do to get better. Reflect with humility and openness and you will be better off for it.

Get-better summary

1. Review is about getting to the method to find the answer; reflection is about improving your core capabilities.
2. The simplest way to reflect is to ask the question, 'Why did I not get that better outcome in the first place?' It is about thinking in hindsight about the activity and understanding what hindered you. And 'I' is crucial to this answer; it cannot begin with 'we' or 'us'.

3. Reflection is not as easy as it seems. When we reflect, we often end up externalizing the problem as opposed to understanding where 'I' need to get better. Use the two techniques of 'specific reflection' and 'outside-in reflection' to avoid that problem.

6

The Pilot's View

Imagine you are part of an orchestra and play a musical instrument, say, the violin. Assume for a moment that the orchestra has over fifty musicians and a conductor. When you are playing the violin, you are immersed in what you are doing, playing the right notes at the right tempo. The orchestra conductor, however, is not evaluating you; they are evaluating the totality of the music being produced and the role your violin is playing in that totality.

In this situation, when you identify the opportunities for you to get better, it will possibly be from the lens of how you need to play the violin better. But if your orchestra conductor were to identify what you need to improve, they would look at what would improve the totality of the music produced by the entire orchestra and hence at what you need to do to improve that totality. *These are two different perspectives and often, as musicians in the orchestra of work and careers, we are unable to see the conductor's perspective and improve ourselves.*

In careers, given that organizations are pyramids and that people higher than us in the pyramid have a wider and more comprehensive view, I like to replace the conductor's view with a pilot's view. I like the analogy where you think that you are driving a bus, but while driving the bus, you must also be able to have a pilot's view from above you to become a better bus driver. The pilot's view is a nice analogy for the perspective of somebody who is higher up in the organizational pyramid than you and I.

An ex-colleague of mine often relates a favourite anecdote. He was a brand manager handling a fledgling product in the overall scheme of things in his company. The primary challenge was how to shift the focus and priority of the organization to a small product. He did many things in terms of strategies and activities to grow that product, but in the absence of that overwhelming organizational buy-in, those activities did not get him anywhere. Then it finally dawned on him that the answer to the problem was not in creating more activity and newer strategies, but in solving the core issue of organizational priority. He realized that to solve the problem of organizational priority, he had to have the pilot's view, not the bus driver's. In a meeting with the CEO of the company, he managed to communicate why that product could make a difference to the entire company, articulate a distinct role for that product that went beyond its small contribution to the current revenue and secure the organizational buy-in that he wanted.

In my days in marketing, I have seen this happen repeatedly—brand managers wanting more resources for the brands and products they are handling. But most of them, when they justify that need for resources, use the bus driver's lens, the lens of what that brand needs. Very few of them get to the pilot's view, describe why that brand is important for the company and why the additional resources are required from that lens.

I have seen the same thing happen in sales as well. There are many geographical regions in our country and sometimes, something might be very important for a particular region, but not be a national priority. When I have visited these markets, the regional manager has often made a passionate pitch for why they need greater support from the company for their regional priorities. Most of the times I have heard that pitch I have probably ignored it, while trying to be empathetic. And that is because the pitch was from a regional lens. If the regional manager instead were to get better and make the pitch from a pilot's view, from my view on how solving the problem for that region could make a difference across the country, then maybe I would have agreed to support more of those pitches.

Many regional sales managers, many brand managers, many factory managers, to quote as examples, suffer from this on a regular basis. Something is important to their brand, factory or region and to them, but because they talk from the bus driver's lens, they are unable to convince their superiors and the company of the importance of that agenda and hence keep getting frustrated. And then they make the same pitch again and again, to the point where sometimes people start joking about it—'Mr X is talking about that again . . .' Unless you can understand and talk from the pilot's viewpoint while being the bus driver, it is unlikely that you will make great progress.

Most people in their careers keep slogging, keep burrowing like the squirrel, without understanding how to make a difference to the big picture. You will have a great career only when what you do makes an impact on the company as a whole. To be able to understand what you need to do to make that impact, you need to get better at developing the pilot's view while being the bus driver. It is a crucial aspect if you want to progress beyond lower and middle-level management to senior management.

However, it is also a very difficult thing to do. That is why I gave it that name—the pilot's view. If you try to visualize it, you can understand that it is not the easiest thing for the bus driver to develop the pilot's view. But if you do want to hit senior management, or if you want to be a successful entrepreneur, then you have to develop that ability. And to do that, you have to practise and adopt specific techniques.

Passenger technique

The bus driver might not get to pilot a plane, but can certainly get to be a passenger on a flight. A passenger in a plane can see the aerial view which they can't when driving a bus. When we work, we also get to be the passengers in a plane sometimes. For instance, in a meeting where your boss is presenting to even more senior people in the organization, you get to see the passenger's view. The important thing is to use that opportunity as a passenger to be able to develop the pilot's view. There are a few things you can do for that:

1. Firstly, listen carefully to what senior managers articulate as important for the company to move ahead. Then evaluate whether your agenda is aligned to those priorities or whether you are like a squirrel, burrowing away on an unimportant agenda. How can you link what you are doing to the company's priorities?
2. Second, when things relevant to your work are being discussed, listen to how the same is being spoken about, which words are used, how it is articulated. Then ask yourself, if you had spoken on the same issue, how would it have been different? The two different articulations would probably reveal the difference of the view from the bus and from the plane. It is about the same topic, but spoken by people who are looking at it from different planes. What would it take for you to articulate your work, your agenda and your issues in the same way your boss and other seniors do?

I often see junior people sitting in such meetings and playing with their phones or sending emails from their laptops. If, as a bus driver, you get to be a passenger on a plane, it is important to look outside the window and understand how the view from a plane is different. It is important to use every opportunity you get to develop that view.

Play the boss

The second technique to develop a pilot's view is to use the opportunity to play the boss—when your boss is on leave and an important situation arises or if he or she deputes you to represent them in an important meeting. Such opportunities do come your way and it is important to use them to build the pilot's view. Prepare for these situations well and while doing so, make a conscious effort to get out of the bus and sit in the plane. That will help you think from a different level and build the right habit.

Thought experiments

What if you don't get the opportunity to be a passenger? What if your boss does not depute you on their behalf? Does that mean you can't develop a pilot's view? These are matters of chance and it is possible that you might not get these opportunities. There is still a third way, which is entirely under your control.

It is about experimenting with your thoughts, thinking about yourself in different situations and starting to develop thoughts on that situation. There are three ways you can do this:

1. Ask yourself, what are the most important drivers for your company? What makes the company succeed and what makes it fail?

2. Put yourself in the shoes of the senior management and ask:
   a. What would you pursue as priorities if you were in their place?
   b. What would you stop doing if you were in their position?
3. Ask yourself different 'what if' questions:
   a. What if your job were eliminated? What impact would it have on the business?
   b. What if you performed brilliantly—would the CEO/MD of the company be positively affected?

These three techniques are useful to develop the pilot's view. I cannot emphasize how important it is to develop this aerial, overarching view. When I observe people who have had moderate or low success, I find that they actually were working hard and with passion, but the issue was that they were doing unimportant things. The pilot's view is important to guide you to work on what makes a difference. The pilot's view also gives you an understanding of which core capabilities to get better at.

An example from my life is when I was in marketing at Asian Paints. At that time, we were advertising many brands, which the team and I, as the person leading that team, were very passionate about. But that was the bus driver's view and we, as a team, were burrowing away behind those multiple brands. A meeting with P.M. Murty, then the president of the company, led me to understand how I was caught up being the bus driver. In that meeting, as my team and I kept pushing the agenda of each of those brands, Mr Murty had a simple rejoinder. He said, 'I don't want to discuss what you are going to do with each brand. Instead, I want to discuss how many brands should we be having and building.' A classic example of the difference between the view from the bus and the plane. That meeting started a project which pruned the number of brands we advertised, the number of growth opportunities we pursued and was immensely beneficial for the future of the business. But independent of what it did for the business, it affected me individually. I realized that I had tremendous passion for what I was doing, but sometimes, in that passion, I failed to ask the core question—is what I am doing actually making a difference? It is important to be passionate about the bus you are driving and drive it with all your heart, but every now and then, you need to have the pilot's view to ask the question 'Are you driving the right bus and are you driving towards the right destination?' Developing the ability to see both views, through the microscope and the telescope, is one of the most important areas to get better in, if you have aspirations of getting to senior management.

Get-better summary

1. To progress from lower and middle management to senior management, it is important to develop the pilot's view while being the bus driver. Passion for what you do does not mean it is important in the big picture. Getting better at seeing the bigger picture

and seeing it from a higher plane is important for long-term success.

2. To develop the pilot's view, one can use the passenger technique effectively. Also, utilizing the chances you get to play the boss and consciously changing your view when you do that will also help you develop the pilot's view. If you don't get the above opportunities, then thought experiments on different scenarios will be useful.

SECTION 2

Getting better is an important factor of long-term success and to get better, it is important to leverage every activity, every project, every day, every hour, without waiting for some special training programme or developmental intervention. That is what I call 'getting better by yourself every hour'.

I explained earlier why it is important to go down to the method and not stop at the answer level. The answer is valid only in that given situation and cannot be extended to other contexts, but the method is applicable in other situations and contexts as well. In the Ajay/Sanjay example, the answer called Shetty's is valid only in that city, but if you know the method to find the answer by locating the nearest transport hub, it is valid across all cities.

In careers and the corporate/entrepreneurship world, most of us get better in the context of a certain domain. This domain is defined by multiple dimensions—the industry we operate in, like FMCG, banking, IT, etc., the functions we operate in, like sales, finance, production, HR, etc. and the geographic regions we operate in. As we work, we keep storing new answers in our heads, but those answers are valid only in the domains we got them in. However, to be successful in your career, you have to be successful across multiple domains. Sometimes, you have to move from one industry to another, sometimes you have to move across functions and many times, you have to move across geographies, even new countries. If you are getting better only to the extent of knowing the answer, then each time you move from one domain to another, you will have to start all over again, and that will limit your career success significantly. If you want to be effective across domains, then you have to get to the method of finding the answer, not stop at the answer itself. Hence, I like to describe the journey of going from the answer to the method of finding the answer as going from domain dependence to domain independence. Only if we make ourselves domain-independent will we experience long-term career success.

In my career, domain independence has been crucial. I have had a successful career, but many people have had more successful careers than mine. However, I do find that the one thing unique about my career is how many domains I have managed to cross and still be successful. I have worked across multiple industry domains like home improvement (paints, waterproofing), consumer durables and FMCG. I have worked across many functional areas like sales, marketing, strategy, HR and general management. I have worked across geographies in India and in the Asia-Pacific. As I mentioned in the introduction, the insight from my own career was that at some stage, I developed a model that was capable of working anywhere. I wanted to analyse when I developed it, why I developed it and how to understand, decode and explain it to others. And now I am clear—that model was based on me not stopping at the answer, but getting to the method of finding the answer, which made me domain-independent. That is what enabled me to cross so many domains. I do hope this inspires you to try very hard to become as domain-independent as possible.

Getting better by leveraging others

In Section 1, I focused on how you can get better yourself based on what you do on a daily basis. Getting better by yourself is exceptionally important to long-term success. However, that is not the only way to get better. There are several resources available, like the people we work with, training programmes and books, among others. These external resources are often very important to accelerate the get-better journey. My own experience has been that most of us do not use these external resources well enough. We think that this happens automatically—e.g., when we attend a training programme, we assume we automatically get better, which is incorrect. Section 2 will deal with how we can leverage other people and all available resources for us to get better:

1. How do you leverage others like your boss and your team in the get-better journey?
2. How do you leverage get-better aids like training programmes, books, etc.?
3. Getting better is not just doing, but also observing others and learning from them.

7

Leveraging Others in Your Organization

I have always been a keen follower of sports and a fairly active sportsperson myself. I feel there is a lot to learn from sports and sportspersons, like resilience, determination, persistence, the ability to perform under pressure and the sportsperson's spirit. One of the biggest differences between a sportsperson and you and me at work is the sportsperson's obsessive focus on getting better—*they spend more time sharpening the axe than cutting the wood, while we spend more time cutting the wood than sharpening the axe*. Some of that is due to the different contexts and can't be helped, but some of it is in our hands.

The other thing I observed about sportspersons that's different from us worker bees is their willingness to take coaching to get better. A sportsperson is willing to let the coach run their lives at times. Saina Nehwal and P.V. Sindhu allowed Pullela Gopichand to literally manage their lives so that he could make them better at badminton. They were willing to take instructions from him that would dictate their lives—when to wake up, which exercises to perform, how much to practise, what to eat, etc. We have heard the same stories about Ramakant Achrekar and Sachin Tendulkar, about Tiger Woods' father and Tiger, and about how the Williams sisters' father made Serena and Venus chase balls that were considered impossible to return.

Two things stand out for me in those stories:

1. The willingness of the sportsperson to take external assistance in the form of a coach in their effort to get better and become world-class. This is far greater than the willingness we show to take external help.
2. The contract between the sportsperson and the coach is very clear—'I want you to make me better and in return, I am willing to do anything you ask me to'. The contract, effectively, is a get-better contract, not a results contract.

As we contextualize it in the work situation, the first observation is that nobody is marked out as a coach. Everybody is a player in the arena of work. Some players are senior players who have played for a long time and occupy higher positions and some are middle/junior players who have just started out. The fact that nobody is just a coach might be why we tend to think that there is no serious external support available to help us get better. This is an incorrect assumption—there is a hell of a lot of external support available to us. This includes our bosses, other seniors and our peers. Even our team, which reports to us, can actually help us get better. Also, in the context of sports, once a player engages a coach, the agenda for improvement is often set by the coach and the player follows it. That is where work is quite different—we have to take the initiative if we want external help. Others are not going to set the agenda and drive it. You want to get better? You drive the agenda!

Leveraging your boss to get better

The single greatest resource you have in your get-better journey is your boss. Your boss can be like a year-long training programme for you as he or she knows you well and can hence customize the training programme to make it work for you. The primary hurdle is that we do not set it up that way. There are a few enlightened bosses who will take it upon themselves to be your training managers, and I have certainly been fortunate to have had them. But the majority will not do it on their own. The onus is upon us to change the nature of the relationship. There are four steps for leveraging your boss to get better—changing the intent, striking the contract, getting to the method to the answers and being very receptive to feedback.

Changing your intent

The starting point to changing that relationship is in the way we view the subordinate–boss dynamic. Currently, the way the average subordinate sees the relationship is: 'I am supposed to produce results and you will push me, cajole me, shout at me and sometimes help me produce those results. Once I produce the results, I will push you, cajole you and even shout at you to help me get the increment and the promotion that I want'. Sorry for being a bit crass about it, but I just want to point out that our relationship with our bosses is very transactional. I do something for you; in return, you do something for me.

What if we were to try and structure that relationship in a more holistic and learning-oriented way? If the intent for us becomes, 'I am supposed to produce results and you will push me, cajole me, shout at me and sometimes help me produce those results. In the journey of producing those results, I also want you to help me get better to produce future results. I want you to make me the best I can be and pass on to me all the skills and knowledge you have acquired in your journey'. Sometimes, it might feel a little idealistic, but believe you me, it is perfectly feasible. Most bosses would love to be put in the seat of a coach by a willing subordinate. But the start has to be about changing the intent for the relationship from our side.

Striking the contract

The second step is to establish a contract with your boss. This is when you have a conversation about the changed intent you have for the relationship. This might feel awkward for you; it might also be awkward for your boss. But trust me, these conversations often result in a positive outcome. One of the greatest joys of being a boss is helping your subordinates get better and grow, and when somebody approaches you with that request, it is fantastic. A key part of this contract is accepting that this does not dilute your need to produce the results or the right of your boss to hold you accountable to that need. When the boss feels this is a smart tactic of getting away with poor performance, they will not play ball. Very few people summon the courage to have this kind of conversation with their bosses. These few who can do it will benefit extraordinarily and will realize that it is not as difficult as it feels.

Getting to the method of finding the answers

We often face situations in which we do not know what to do and need our boss's help. In such instances, we go to the boss, explain the situation and ask what we should do. The boss usually provides us with a solution—'Go do this'—and we walk away with that answer.

These situations are perhaps the greatest underleveraging of our bosses; when we did not know an answer, we got the answer and simply walked away with it. This is the time to stop and ask, 'Boss, could you please explain to me the method by which you arrived at this answer?' If we just walk away with the answer, then we are only resolving that situation; we are not getting better. It is only when we get to the method of finding the answer that we get better and learn from the boss. There is a difference between *push* and *pull* information. Answers are pushed to us; but the method of finding the answer, we have to pull that out.

Being receptive to feedback

Bosses often have important feedback to give us to make us better. Sometimes, this is a part of formal processes like appraisals and feedback sessions. Sometimes, it is informal and happens on the spot or over one-on-ones in the normal course of work. The get-better feedback from your boss is gold dust—it is crucial to receive it and internalize it.

At times you may be quite defensive, somewhat emotional and quite difficult to give feedback to. Put yourself in your boss's shoes in this situation. The boss is thinking, 'I am going to manage this subordinate for a few years. Why should I give honest feedback and then go through the pain of an adverse, defensive reaction? That person might even quit because of adverse feedback. I don't want to take the unpleasantness and the risk, so let me just paper over the real get-better issues, give some bland feedback and get past this year.' Some of you who have been bosses have possibly experienced this situation and have actually backed off from giving honest feedback to such people.

Now return to your shoes and honestly assess—whose loss is it? If you are difficult and defensive while receiving feedback from your boss, feedback that will make you try and get better, why would they bother to give it? The answer is clear—you have lost an opportunity to get truly valuable feedback that helps you identify areas for improvement.

Giving feedback is as challenging as receiving feedback, if not more. If we make that process difficult for our bosses, then they will take the easy way out and not give us truly honest and important feedback. Be an easy person to give feedback to. You don't have to accept everything that is said, but if you don't make it easy, many things might not even be said, and that is your loss.

In summary, bosses can help you get to the method of finding the answers by passing their knowledge on to you. The feedback of your boss is crucial to building your core capabilities as they have a great understanding of your strengths and weaknesses.

Sometimes, you end up with a poor boss—it can happen to any of us. Does that mean you don't leverage that person? There is a lot one can learn even from a bad boss. There are three kinds of bad bosses. The first kind is one who is not capable when seen through the lens of a business role, but is a good human being. The second is the opposite—highly capable through a business lens, but a difficult human being. The third type is one whose both aspects are unfavourable. I think there is a lot to learn from the first two types. Nobody is perfect, you and I are not perfect, so why do we need a perfect boss to leverage and learn from?

Leveraging your team to get better

If you have a team reporting to you, leverage them to get better. The principles remain the same.

The first is that when they come to you asking for a solution to a problem, don't stop at just giving them the answer; also give them the method of finding the answer. This will make both you and your team better.

It is important to understand why this will make you better. Having worked for many years, I know that there are many answers we pick up from simply having gone through that situation many times in the past. That does not mean we ourselves know the method of finding the answer. Hypothetically, if I know the answers to 100 situations, there are probably 30–40 situations in which I know the answer without knowing the method of finding the answer. Each time I give an answer to a subordinate, if I can explain my method, I will become much better. And many times, that discussion about the method might result not only in you discovering the method but also in actually improving the method.

The second is the get-better feedback from your team. While there are many processes for our bosses to give us feedback, there are fewer processes for feedback from our teams. Our bosses will give us feedback without us asking for it; our teams will not give us feedback unless we explicitly ask them, 'Tell me what you think I need to get better at'. I have always personally practised this—as a ritual, at the end of any appraisal discussion, I have always asked for feedback on myself. And that opinion has helped me immensely in leadership development.

Let me explain why getting better feedback from your team is important for you. In any organization, there are three stakeholder groups we have to be effective with—the people above us (our boss and seniors), people beside us (our peers) and people below us (our teams and their teams). Let us say we have to distribute 100 points between these entities based on the importance of our being effective with them. For instance, if you think it is most important to be effective with the people above you, and then with your team, and then with your peers, then maybe your allocation of the points is fifty, thirty and twenty, respectively. Now that you have understood the concept, I want you to complete an exercise. I want you to allocate the 100 points to those three stakeholder groups for four different situations:

1. Situation One: You are a junior, with 0–5 years of total working time
2. Situation Two: You are middle management, with 12–18 years of total working time
3. Situation Three: You are senior management, with 20–30 years of total working time
4. Situation Four: You are the CEO

Take a few minutes and allocate those 100 points to the three stakeholder groups. Please do so in the sequence I have written—Situation One first and Situation Four last.

As you perform the exercise, the pattern will become obvious to you. As you go from junior to senior, two things happen:

1. Your boss is the most important stakeholder for you when you are a junior person. However, the importance of the people above you keeps decreasing as you become senior.
2. The importance of being effective with the people below you keeps increasing as you become senior.

And when you become the CEO, the only group you have to be effective with is the people below you.

Hence it is obvious that to be successful, over time, we have to become highly effective with the people below us, not just with the people above us. However, some habits become a barrier to this. When we are juniors, we form a habit of getting feedback from our bosses because we want to be effective with them. We do not form the habit of obtaining get-better feedback from people below us. Unfortunately, that habit does not change even as we hit middle and senior management, despite the fact that now, being effective with people below us is much more important. How can one be effective with a group if we don't even bother to get active feedback from them? And to get that feedback, we have to ask for it; it won't come by itself.

Get-better summary

1. Sportspersons leverage coaches and other resources in their journey towards continuously getting better. You and I do not show the same attitude towards leveraging others.
2. Within the organization, the key people you can leverage to get better are your boss, other seniors, your team and the people below you.
3. Your boss is like a customized year-long training programme for you if you can set it up that way. The key steps to that are having the right intent,

establishing the contract, not stopping at just getting the answers but getting the method to the answers too and lastly, making it easy for the boss to give feedback.

4. With your team, the steps to getting better are not just giving them answers, but giving them the method to the answers and directly seeking get-better feedback from them. As you go from being junior to senior, the importance of being highly effective with people below you keeps increasing, and if you don't actively seek feedback from them, you are not going to get better as a leader.

8

Learning by the Book

Has a training program changed your life? Mine has. A few years ago, I was fortunate to be nominated for a coveted signature training programme in my past company. I remember going to that programme and coming back shaken. I realized that the stressed-out, intensely driven way in which I worked was not sustainable, and I would experience burnout soon, leading to multiple health challenges. That programme was a turning point in my life—it completely changed the approach I had towards work. It taught me that great success without physical and mental well-being was of no use; it taught me to work hard without being stressed out (some of my subordinates joked that I stopped 'taking stress' and instead, became an expert at 'giving stress' to others!). A training programme can sometimes change your life.

Has a book impacted your career success positively? It has for me. Way back in 1996 I read *The 7 Habits of Highly Effective People* by Stephen Covey. A single concept in that book—the circle of influence and the circle of concern—brought about another major change in my life. I can confidently say that a lot of success in the first half of my career came from my ability to focus on where I could make a difference and ignore what was beyond my influence. Hence, no situation fazes me—I concentrate only on what I can do in that situation, not on the odds against me.

In recent times, I have spoken to various people and one of the things I ask them to do is describe the 'change events' in their lives and careers. Seldom do I hear answers like the ones I have described above—a training intervention or a book. It made me think that possibly, most people are not using these interventions well in their get-better journey. I do want you to reflect for a brief while on whether any training programme or book has made a significant difference in your career and life.

Firstly, I want to emphasize how valuable books and training programmes are in your get-better journey. To give a sporting analogy again, a player improves in two ways; one, during the game itself, through self-review, reflection and getting better by themselves, and the second, during practice between games, often with the assistance of others. A training programme or a book is like the practice session for us corporate players. In a practice session, a player has only a get-better objective, they do not have a results objective. The same thing applies to us when in a training programme or when reading a book. We can be single-minded about getting better using these interventions without worrying about producing results.

I did establish in earlier chapters that getting better by yourself based on day-to-day work is the single most important thing in your get-better journey. I do maintain that, but doing that without the help of training and books can be suboptimal. Getting better by yourself produces a linear get-better graph. It is a continuous improvement journey. Training programmes and books are like the step jumps to that linear graph. They are inflection points. Just a linear curve without inflection points will be ineffective in the long term and, hence, it is important to leverage books and training programmes.

Knowing is different from embedding

The primary reason most people do not leverage these to create inflections is because they confuse knowing the content with embedding it in their behaviours and lives. Just because you attended the training programme or read the book, and now know its content, does not mean that you have embedded it and changed yourself as a result. I want you to perform an exercise—think of the last book you read and now write down, 'How have you changed as a result of having read the book? What are you doing today that you would not have done if you had not read the book?'

I have often wondered—millions of people have read Stephen Covey's book, but have all of them experienced the inflection change like I did? If they did not experience it, it was not because they read different content. *The difference was not in knowing the content; the difference was in what I did to change myself afterwards as a result of knowing the content.*

To create inflection changes, our focus must not be only on reading the book or attending the training programme. Our focus has to be strongly on what we are doing after reading the book or attending the programme. Reading a book is like having a diet plan to lose weight. Just having the plan does not produce results—you have to implement it.

Getting better through training programmes

When I was in HR, I noticed that in many of the training programmes, there were last-minute dropouts. It used to freak me out. I would think, here we are, as a company, giving employees an opportunity to forget about producing results for a few days and instead focus only on their improvement. And yet they don't want such an opportunity! I often thought of scrapping all training because I thought that if the people getting trained were not interested, why should the company bother?

The starting point to leveraging training is intent and discipline. You are getting a few days just to get better, with no results objectives—it is like practice time for a sportsperson, with no match pressure. A few more days of results do not have the potential to create a positive change event in your life and career, but a few days of a training programme do. Grab every opportunity that comes your way, and bring all your intent and seriousness to it.

The Friday/Monday syndrome

The other key reason for why training programmes are ineffective is the Friday/Monday syndrome. Most training programmes end on Fridays since companies have a tendency to schedule these in the latter half of the week. On Friday evening, the attendees are fully enthused, with new ideas and thoughts of improvement. But on Monday, when they get back to work, they change nothing. If, as a consequence of attending the training, your actions on Monday have not changed from what they would have been on Friday, there is no chance that the training will have a positive impact on you. *The single most important way to exploit training is to change the very next day*. If you postpone the change to sometime in the future, it has a very low chance of being carried out.

The other way to think about this is to go back to your student days. You were explained some concepts by the teacher in the classroom. Most of us did not stop at that—we spent time solving problems based on those concepts outside the classroom through self-study, homework or assignments. If you had only listened to it in the class, and done no practice afterwards, in all probability, you would not have learnt the concept. A training programme is like a classroom—if we don't follow the class with practice, then the class has no impact.

To be able to follow up, we should be able to identify the most important get-better opportunities in the training programme. A good way to do that is to go to the patterns your reflections have been throwing up, the core capabilities you need to get better at. If you can connect the need from your reflections to something you learnt from the training programme, you are fulfilling a real need. Pick that concept from the training and then start to implement it from the next day onwards.

Getting better through books

The core principle of getting better from reading a book is the same as that for a training programme. Knowing the content does not mean you are embedding it. The Friday/Monday syndrome applies to books also. Unless you make a deliberate plan to change yourself in some areas after reading a book, there is no significant benefit of reading it. Having said that, there are nuances to leveraging a book, and I want to highlight some of them.

Firstly, when you read a book, it often represents the distilled wisdom of the kind of people you might never get to interact with in real life. It is as if some truly exceptional people are making their insights available to you to learn from for just a few hundred rupees or a few dollars. As a youngster, reading Jack Welch or Bill Gates or Mahatma Gandhi was like having these people personally sit and coach me to get better, something which was impossible otherwise.

An important thing we have to change in the way we read a book is the time we take to finish it. You can take three months to read a novel, going back to it only when you have leisure, at your own pace. But self-help books and business books need to be read faster. If you read it over a very lengthy period, you lose the ability to connect across the chapters and make sense of them. I do recommend that you read these books within a few weeks.

The second point is the amount of time you spend reading compared to the time you spend imbibing the change. I notice that several people finish one book and start the next immediately—that is not going to help. If you don't spend time internalizing the content from the first book, it is time wasted. In the classroom and practice analogy I gave, this would be like going to classes, without devoting any time to practise. For each book you read, you need to make a plan to get better using it and ideally, not start the next book until you have made some progress with your plan from the previous book. There has to be a difference between the way we read a storybook and a self-help or management book. We don't read self-help and management books for entertainment, but to improve, and you can do that only if you focus on imbibing what you have read.

The third point is to know the content well. Not everything in a book is relevant to you at the time you read it. However, that does not mean that those parts won't be relevant later, in another situation. Hence, even if it's not all relevant right away, understanding everything in a book and having the discipline to come back to it later is a great way to exploit a book fully for self-improvement.

The above principles are difficult to apply for all the books you read. Hence, as an approach, I recommend that you read fewer books. But the books you do read, you must know well, and also spend time applying the learning from them. You will realize that some books resonate deeply with you and that you can get better reading them. Please do make a special effort to master those few books and convert them from one-time reads to lifelong coaching experiences.

The principles that I described for getting better using training programmes and books apply to other kinds of learning interventions as well. It might be an online programme or video content—the nature of the programme does not matter. The same get-better principles have to be applied to gain from them.

Books and training programmes change your core capabilities; they are not situation-specific. And that is why it is crucial to leverage them.

Get-better summary

1. Books and training programmes have the potential to become change events in your get-better journey. Getting better by yourself normally results in continuous learning and a linear curve. Books and training can create step jumps and inflection points in that curve.
2. To leverage them, it is important that you go beyond knowing the content to embedding the content—avoid the Friday/Monday syndrome. Be it a training programme or a book, make a list of things you want to imbibe and create time, space and discipline to embed them. Start the imbibing process from the next day—don't postpone it.

3. To fully utilize a book, it is important to read it at a fair pace. A book read over many months is unlikely to make you better as you lose the links between chapters. Some of the content may not be relevant right away, but might be useful to a situation you face in the future. You must know the content well to be able to come back to it when required.
4. Books and training programmes improve your core capabilities and that is why they are crucial to getting better.

SECTION 3

In Section 1, we covered the method of getting better by ourselves by doing the day-to-day stuff, using every hour and every activity. The means to that was adopting review and reflection and developing the pilot's view.

In Section 2, we covered how to leverage others to get better. The key areas we covered are:

1. How to leverage others in your organization—your bosses and your team.
2. How to leverage interventions likes books, training programmes, etc. to drive change in your get-better journey.

There is also another method of getting better that integrates these two approaches. It leverages others as well as the process of getting better by yourself. This method is called getting better by observation, as opposed to getting better by action. If you look at both Section 1 and Section 2, it is about getting better based on what you do. Getting better by observation changes that paradigm and moves on to how can you improve based on what others do, and which you observe.

Let us take an outlandish example to make it interesting. Let us say you observe the prime minister or the president of your country do something. You can see the action they have taken, their decision, but you don't have access to the reasons for that decision. Put simply, it is equivalent to knowing the answer, not the method of finding the answer. Here, you would need to apply review, reflection and pilot's view. That will help you understand what the impact of that action was, what could have been done better and also, from a pilot's view, why it was done. This will help you get better based on what they have done.

The same thing can be applied to anything important you observe at work. It could be a new product launch by a competitor, a senior leader setting a new priority or a project that somebody in another vertical of your organization is doing. You can get better based on what they did by observing and then applying review, reflection and pilot's view.

This technique is particularly important for the younger, junior people. Let us go to the junior-most person, a trainee or intern. As a trainee or intern, there are limited things you can do, but the ocean of what you observe others doing is vast. At this stage, if you learn only from what you do, then it can be quite limiting because what you do is quite small in the overall context of the business. Hence, it is important to learn from what others do, the actions the company is taking, what seniors in the organization are doing, etc. to further accelerate your improvement.

An example of getting better by observation is how I enhanced my marketing skills. An obvious way to get better at marketing was using what I did and learning from that. But another very potent method for me was learning by being a consumer. As a consumer, I was exposed to a lot of marketing targeted at me. Whenever I found that the marketing by some brand—it could be clothing, automobiles, smartphones—made an impact on me, I observed. I would ask myself why that brand used that particular marketing strategy. Why did it affect me? What could they have done to get an even better outcome? In a way, I was using review, reflection and pilot's view on the marketing actions taken by brands and people I did not know, and getting better based on it.

Both Section 1 and Section 2 focus on making you better. However, Section 3 goes beyond trying to make you better, to making others better.

I am sure you're wondering how making others better helps you get better. I agree, it does not help you directly, but it helps you achieve the same results that you get when you focus on self-improvement.

Our focus in Sections 1 and 2 has been on getting better so that we get much better results and success for the same effort. Now, if you ask what else you can do to achieve the same objective, besides getting better, you will immediately realize that making others in your ecosystem better will also help you improve your results, for the same effort.

In modern corporations and businesses, none of us exist in isolation—we all have ecosystems that help us produce results. The most important part of your ecosystem is your team, the people who work for you. If you help them get better, then the results you produce for a given amount of your effort will increase significantly. There is also an external ecosystem that all of us have. E.g., if you are in HR, your external ecosystem comprises recruitment agencies, training companies, HR IT and payroll companies, etc. If you are in finance, your external ecosystem comprises auditors, ERP software vendors, outsourced partners, etc. If you are in sales, your external ecosystem comprises your distributors, the outsourced sales force and your retailers. If you are a dentist, your external ecosystem comprises people who supply dentures, X-rays, etc.

Just reflect for a moment on what would happen to the results you produce if each of these ecosystem partners became twice as good as they are right now. Yet, most people don't understand this and hence, do not put enough effort into making others better. If all your focus is on you getting better, you are still leaving a lot of money on the table in your ecosystem. Some part of your effort must also go towards making others better.

The direct payoff to making others better is obvious: it improves your results for a given amount of effort from you. There is also an indirect payoff, and that is the goodwill and leadership you generate from those you helped. That goodwill and leadership will also have a longer-term payoff and benefit beyond just the short-term results. Hence, Section 3 will cover techniques of making others better. The two significant others we will cover are your direct team and your external ecosystem partners.

9

Making Your Team Better

When I look back at my most successful periods, it's clear that there was a very high correlation between my success and how good my teams were in that phase. I have always been reasonably effective myself in most of my stints, barring a few. Yet, my success and my results were not consistent over all the stints where I was personally effective; a lot of that was due to how much my team was multiplying my efforts. In some roles, my teams were greatly multiplying my efforts, while in others, that multiplication factor was weak and the overall difference in results was obvious. This reinforced my belief in making my teams better and for many years now, I have always placed a significant emphasis on this aspect. Each one of us needs to understand that the biggest gainer in making our teams better is us. Hence, it is worth our time and our attention to prioritize making our teams get better.

To make your team better, there are two things you can do. The first is hiring better, which is about getting the right person into the team, and the second is about making the existing team better through your interactions and development inputs. I will cover both aspects in this chapter.

Hiring well

The starting point to making your team better is to ensure that you induct the right people at the point of hiring. Hiring as a process is given inadequate attention. We tend to think it is HR's problem to hire. HR has a role to play, but the biggest benefit of hiring well accrues to us. I often find that people are so caught up in their daily jobs that they do not give the hiring process the time, the attention and the priority it deserves. We don't take out those few extra hours required to hire the right person because we are doing a hundred other things. Later, we suffer over thousands of hours because of a poor hiring decision. A few hours saved can result in a thousand hours wasted later. So please, do not be stingy with the time and the focus you give to hiring.

The key to hiring well is to reconsider and change what you are looking for in the prospective candidate. Most of us ask questions in interviews and then see if the candidate has the right answers. Instead, we have to try and discern if the candidate has a method of finding the answers. Secondly, most of us check if the candidate is currently successful. Instead, we have to shift to assessing if the candidate has a superior GBM, which assures future success.

In most interviews there is one standard question that is asked: 'Tell us about a major achievement in your last job.' And the candidate gives an excellent answer describing an important achievement and its impressive results. Results can be due to many reasons—because the candidate had a great boss, the circumstances were favourable and so on. The results are not what the person carries into the new job you are hiring for. What the person will carry into the job is the method of producing the results and the core capabilities developed while producing those results. In most interviews, the questions stop at the results and don't dive deeper into understanding whether the person has a superior method of finding the answers, or has developed capabilities that are useful in the context of the new job.

The second thing I have seen people look for in interviews is how successful the candidate is in their current and previous assignments. There is a belief that if a candidate was successful in their previous job, they will succeed in the next job, too. Success, again, can be due to a combination of circumstances and the ecosystem. While past success is highly desirable in a candidate, it is more important to check for the capability for future success, and that is about checking how good the GBM of the candidate is, their model to keep getting better.

My interview strategy

Once I understood this, I changed my own hiring approach. Here is what I do nowadays in a hiring situation: Before going into an interview, I study the candidate's

CV thoroughly. The CV usually states what they have done in the past—that is not going to be useful to me in the future. What I am interested in is the methods to finding answers they have developed and how good their response to future situations will be. Hence, I don't ask questions like 'What did you do in your previous job?', 'Tell me about your achievements', etc. Instead, based on their CV, I present to them some future scenarios that I think will be important in my business, and ask them how they will respond to those situations. My hypothesis is simple—I already know what you have done. If you have indeed got better in that process, you should be able to respond better to similar future situations that I pose to you. In a way, this is testing a person's ability to find the answers to future situations and the core capabilities they have developed. Past answers are not useful to me; the ability to find the answers in the future is what I need to check for.

Sometimes, despite me not specifically asking the question, the interview organically flows into a candidate's achievements. I usually have two follow-up questions:

1. What did you learn from those achievements?
2. How will those learnings help in the job you have applied for?

Sometimes, I ask people to do a live review in the interview. They state something they have done and I ask, 'What could you have done to get a better outcome than what you achieved in that situation?' It is amazing to see that there are so many people who are unable to give quality answers to these follow-up questions.

I strongly recommend that you also change your hiring strategy to drive the following fundamental shifts:

From	**To**
Looking for the right answers for the questions you ask	Looking for the method to the answers
Assessing past success	Assessing core capabilities for future success

In effect, change your hiring strategy to hire people with better GBMs.

This shift is particularly crucial when you hire people across domains, be it industry domains, geographical domains or functional domains. When people get hired into the same domain, they can get away with knowing the answers without knowing the methods to the answers, but when you hire from a new domain, say from a different industry, the past answers are not applicable. What is useful is the method of finding the answer and the core capabilities, and that is what you must hire for.

As I wrote this chapter, I actually made a list of the last fifteen people I have hired. Fourteen of them have gone on to do remarkably well in their careers and lives—a reaffirmation of my hiring strategy and a source of happiness.

Lastly, this method is applicable even when you select candidates from within your company for a role. What you are looking for does not change—you are assessing their GBM. How you do that might not be through an interview, but by other methods. Follow the same principles, whatever be the hiring source.

Getting hired

This brings us to a question which is probably playing on a lot of readers' minds—will this also help me get hired? It goes without saying that if these techniques help you to hire well, these should also help you get hired and crack the interviews you go to.

When you are asked questions in an interview, don't stop at the answer—go on to showcase the underlying ability you have developed in getting to that answer, and how that ability will help the hiring company. For instance, at the end of my Asian Paints stint in 2000, if somebody asked me in an interview, 'What was your biggest achievement at Asian Paints?' my answer would go something like this:

1. One of my big contributions was in moving the company from an interior paints company to an interior and exterior paints company. I did this by nurturing a fledgling Apex exterior emulsion and growing it strongly, and by launching a product called Ace exterior emulsion.
2. In doing that, I developed the capability to create categories and new businesses. This was not about taking market share from other exterior paints, but

about fundamentally creating a new market where none existed before. I built that capability through my experience with exteriors in Asian Paints.

3. My ability to create categories and a new market would help your business in the following possible ways: ______________________________

Most people, when asked about their achievements, stop at point one. Everybody who comes to an interview has an answer up until point one, so if you stop at that level, there is nothing differentiating you from other candidates. Instead, if you go to points two and three, you are going to look far better and have a greater chance of being hired. Don't stop at giving the answers; showcase your method of getting to the answers, the capabilities you developed and how those would benefit the hiring company.

Sometimes, the interviewer might not have the skills to ask you those questions. Don't be discouraged and answer only what is asked. Using the right opportunities, steer the conversation to what you want to share. That is what will get you hired.

Making your existing team better

Apart from hiring well, the other crucial thing you have to do relates to making your current team better.

As bosses, we have many interactions with our teams daily. It could be meetings, reviews or field visits—the important thing is to use every interaction to help them get better. We should not think that helping the team get better is only about special interactions like appraisals; it is a daily job.

The simplest technique I have found to help them get better is to push for clarity on the 'why'. Your team will often come and talk to you about what they want to do. My question is always about why they want to do it, what problem they are trying to solve and establishing clarity on that. When I push them to explain the 'why', the conversation automatically strengthens their method of developing the answer. If they only had the answer and not the method of finding the answer, they would not be able to answer the 'why' question well.

Let me give an example of this. Often, teams get excited by new product ideas, which they then bring to me. My typical line of conversation would be:

1. What is the consumer problem we are solving with this new product?
2. Why can't one of our existing products solve the same problem? Why do we need a new product?
3. Why do you prioritize this over other initiatives in the business?

Questions like these, and the resulting conversation, force the team to go beyond the idea, to the 'why', and that is where they start developing their method of finding the answers.

The second technique to helping improve your team is to set high standards of 'what is good'. When you consistently set high standards, they are automatically forced to get better to meet those standards. Sometimes, high standards can be confused with high targets. High standards are about your definition of 'good'. When your bar for 'good' is set high, then the teams have to strive and get better to reach that bar; it is a very powerful way of making them better. The challenge with this, however, is managing motivation. Having high standards can make the team feel like their work is not appreciated, or give rise to a general feeling of not being good enough. I have often struggled to walk that thin line. To use this technique, you must always be very aware of the thin line, and not topple over to the wrong side.

The third technique is formal training. I have myself conducted many sessions as a trainer for my teams. I started this in Onida, where I did several sessions on planning and marketing and advertising for the teams. I did the 'Tee off with Mouli' sessions in Cadbury to help people succeed. In Pidilite, I started a concept called Master Class, where other seniors and I spent a lot of time training the teams. While leveraging daily interactions to make the team better is important, the step jumps often come when we are willing to commit time and energy to the more formal training programmes which we are willing to lead. So go ahead and make that effort.

The last, but not the least, way to help your team get better is to use organizational processes like appraisals, career planning, potential planning, development planning, etc. to the maximum effect. If, as a manager, you do true justice to these activities, you will really help your team get better. I have personally put massive time and effort into doing appraisals well. A simple rule of the thumb I had was that if I had set ninety minutes aside for an appraisal conversation, I should spend at least ninety minutes preparing for that conversation. And the feedback I gave was always structured on the 'what' and 'how'. The 'what' covered areas I think they handled well, and where they could have done better. This could be about results, specific activities, performance against goals, etc. However, I did not stop there. I always went to the 'how'. The 'how' was about their method to the answer, their core capabilities which resulted in the performance they delivered. I would give my hypothesis on what enabled them to perform well in some areas and what capability issues prevented them from performing well in others. When you stop at saying that you did not do well in an area, that is judgement. That judgement does not help your team member deduce how to get better. To help them progress, it is important to also give your opinion on the reasons they did not do well in that area. *The purpose of an appraisal conversation is not to pass judgement, but to give feedback to help them get better.*

My journey as a boss

I have learnt a lot from my journey as a boss. People have always regarded me as a tough boss—uncompromising, setting high standards and sometimes being quite painful in implementing those standards. By any yardstick, I am not a very easy person to work with. Yet, I have seen very low attrition among the people who have worked with me. There was once a period of twelve years in which not a single person who was in my team voluntarily quit the company. The only change was when they moved to other jobs within the company. I reflected on these two contradictory aspects—a tough boss with zero attrition. The reason became clear—people stayed with me because I was very good at helping them get better.

As a boss, when you are tough and uncompromising even in challenging circumstances, the extent to which people accept you depends a lot on your values and your intent. If the team feels that the boss is tough for his own selfish reasons, that he wants to show great results and get a promotion or a new job, they don't accept the toughness—they might quit or take other actions. But if they feel the boss is tough because it is in the interest of the company or because it is in their interest as it makes them better, they are highly committed and loyal. That is what was happening in my case—people knew I was painfully tough, but they also had the confidence that I was not doing it for selfish reasons, but because it was in their best interests and in the interests of the company.

I did have a selfish reason, though. I knew that when I make my team better, the greatest gain comes to me. Your team multiplies your efforts and your results. Hence, making them better is an important priority. As you do that, there is also the goodwill you generate, which gets you long-term commitment from people. To make people better, sometimes, you have to be tough, you have to push, you have to set challenging standards. People will accept this from you only if they respect your intent and your values. A tough boss with a selfish intent and poor values is the most destructive of all bosses—they are certain to destroy their teams, and even the company, in the long term. Making the team better is the objective, the intent, and values are the licence to attempt that.

Get-better summary

1. To be successful, you must make your team better. The biggest benefit of a team getting better accrues to the boss.
2. To make the team better, you have to change your hiring strategy:
    a. From looking for the right answers to your questions to looking for the methods to finding the answers.
    b. From looking for past success to looking for the GBM that predicts success in the future.
3. The same technique helps you get hired. Don't stop at giving the answer to a question; show them how you have built capabilities in getting to that answer and how those capabilities can make a difference to the new assignment.
4. To make your existing team better, there are four techniques you can use:
    a. Focus on the 'why'.
    b. Set high standards which force them to get better. Do not misinterpret setting high standards as a licence to setting high and unreasonable targets.
    c. Make the effort to drive formal training where you are the trainer.

   d. Leverage company processes like appraisals and development planning to make a difference to the teams.

5. If you are trying to make the team better for your selfish gain, they will not accept it. The greatest gain from helping your team get better comes to you, but the right intent and values are the licence you require for that.

10

Leveraging the External Ecosystem

Many years back, when I was the head of marketing at Cadbury, I conducted a session for the younger people in the marketing team. One of the questions up for debate was how to become a good marketer. There were many responses, some of which were:

1. Work hard.
2. Be creative and innovative.
3. Ensure sound analytics.
4. Have a good understanding of the consumer.

I could go on and fill the page with the many answers, but there was a pattern in all the answers—they were all about what marketers needed to do.

I then explained what it took for me to be a good marketer. I said, 'Find a good advertising agency, find a good media agency, find a good digital agency, find a good market research partner, find a good film producer, find a good activation agency: cultivate and nurture them, and you are already three-fourths of the way on your journey to be a good marketer.' My answer is all about external partners who contribute to a marketer's success and effectiveness. And yet, when we think about being effective, we think of only the internal, within the business; we don't think of how to be effective in leveraging external partners. Getting better at leveraging the external partners is critical to long-term success, not just in marketing, but in all fields.

Between 2010 and 2013, Cadbury/Mondelez India was awarded the Effie Client of the Year two years in a row as well as the Emvies Client of the Year. For those of you who don't come from a marketing background, these are awards given by the Advertising Club of Mumbai annually. Winning these awards meant that our company was recognized as the best marketing company of the year across all companies and industries. Without a doubt, a major reason behind this recognition was that we had a fantastic marketing team within the company, but an even bigger reason was that we had a fantastic set of external partners and agencies—what I refer to as the marketing ecosystem. We got awarded as the best marketing company because we were very good at assembling the best external partners and in getting the best out of them during those years.

The logic for making the external ecosystem better remains the same. For the same effort from us, a better external partner ecosystem will get us better results. All parts of the business have an external ecosystem, not only marketing. Procurement has to work with vendors, HR with training companies and recruitment companies, IT works with software vendors, finance with auditors and tax advisors, sales with distributors and the outsourced sales force, logistics with C&F agencies and transporters, and so on. In any role, map the external ecosystem you have and then ask yourself the first question—what would be the impact on you if that external ecosystem improved significantly? And when you conclude that there is a significant positive impact on your results if they get better, ask the second question—what are *you* doing to help them get better?

You probably think that since they are external to us, we have no role in helping them progress. That is incorrect. We can play a significant role in their enhancement, and therefore in their effectiveness for our business. There are three ways we can help make them better for our business:

1. Move from vendor to partnership mindset.
2. Enable them to upgrade their people and capabilities with the right remuneration.
3. Leadership role modelling.

From vendor to partner

In many cases, external partners don't perform even up to their current potential. They provide the same service to several clients, with your business being just one of them. It is quite possible that the quality of work and services for your business is much lower than what they provide other clients. It is, then, not about making them better overall, but more about getting the best out of them even at their current potential.

This requires a fundamental change in our mindset—the change of treating external entities not as vendors but as partners, and building a partnership as opposed to a buyer–seller relationship. There are two kinds of external vendors—first, where what they sell is commoditized and can be measured against specifications, and second, where there is some amount of customization and value addition in each transaction. An example of the first type is, say, sugar for a food company or oil for a refinery or pigment for a paint company. An example of the second type is legal advice for a specific problem from a lawyer, or an advertising agency, or a training company.

We usually end up engaging with all kinds of external vendors in the traditional buyer–seller relationship, where the buyer sets the specifications and the terms, then negotiates the best price, and the seller then fulfils the agreed requirements. However, for the more customized and value-add vendors, something more collaborative and closer to a partnership creates better long-term value. We are not buying something from them, but often co-creating, and that requires a partnership orientation.

There are four main practices required to build the partnership orientation:

1. While the buyer pays for the services, they should not behave like one on a day-to-day basis. In routine

engagement, it must be a relationship of equality, not a buyer–seller relationship.
2. Instead of telling the vendor what to do, involve them in the resolution of the problem.
3. Give them a sense of ownership.
4. Recognize and celebrate their contribution.

The simple act of changing the relationship from a vendor to a partnership mode will help you get much better output from your external ecosystem, which will help boost your results.

Right capability through right remuneration

To help your external partner deliver good service to you, it is important to help them have the right quality of people facing your business. Mindless negotiation in a competitive environment often results in the partner having to compromise on the quality of the people to make ends meet. In modern organizations, the procurement function is often involved in the negotiation and purchase of all services. And the procurement function approach is usually to reduce all services to a commodity and then negotiate. While that might save some money in the service itself, the overall impact it has on the business results could be quite bad, as lower rates means poor quality of people at the partner firm.

I want to give an example of where I helped one of my external partners get better by improving the quality of their people. To be able to do that, I changed the remuneration model from a fixed fee. Instead, I split the fee into two components—one component was the cost of the people they deployed to my business, and the second was the overheads and profit margin. We negotiated to fix the second component, but for the first component, which was about the people they deployed to my business, I changed the model completely to a reimbursement of actuals as opposed to a fixed amount. In a way, I liberated them from constraints on what they paid their people and encouraged them to hire the best for my business. This move enabled my ecosystem partner to hire the best in the industry and hence they got much better people and helped us produce fantastic results over the next few years.

Leadership role modelling

The interesting thing I am observing is that slowly but surely, in many of the buyer–seller relationships, the buyers are starting to invest energy into making their external ecosystems better. Nowhere is this exemplified better than in the traditional procurement or purchase function, where earlier, the primary task was to squeeze the best rates and terms out of the seller. Nowadays, the bulk of the procurement job is about helping the vendors deliver better, be it through strategic sourcing, quality audits, co-development of new products and packaging, etc. In a sales function, much of the sale force is often outsourced to an external partner or a distributor. In that kind of situation, if you did not invest time and effort into making your distributor better, you might not get a lot of success. Making the external ecosystem better has to be a priority for us. The interesting thing is that even the customers, at times, can be treated as part of the external ecosystem, and efforts can be made to make them better. In Pidilite, while the carpenter is the customer for the Fevicol brand, the company makes a significant and regular effort to upgrade their skills and capabilities. These are all examples of people making efforts to make the external ecosystem better, which is a key part of success.

I have noticed that this is often driven by the cultural dynamic created by the leaders. When leaders model the behaviours that vendors must not be treated as vendors but as partners, that culture often flows down the organization. I was fortunate that in my formative years, I saw my mentor, Bharat Puri, perform this role at Asian Paints, and it became ingrained in me. In another organization, I saw that the leader was very transactional with the vendors. Hence the entire organization started following that culture, thus not getting the best from the external partners. I have personally practised having top-to-top meetings with my partners without any specific business agenda, focused on how we can create value together.

One of the great ecosystems built in recent times is the app ecosystem that Apple built for its iPhone. A large number of independent app developers have built apps and sold them to customers through the iPhone app store. In a way, the ecosystem of app developers worked towards making the iPhone successful. They were not selling something to iPhone, but as ecosystem partners, they were working hard to make the iPhone successful. The more the ecosystem succeeded, the more iPhone succeeded. The same is the case with the Android ecosystem as well. Possibly, in a previous era, a company would have structured this as a buyer–seller relationship, bought apps from the ecosystem and sold them to customers. Do you think that model would have been equally successful?

The successful companies and individuals in the future will be those who can leverage their ecosystems as force multipliers and not as vendors and suppliers. The most important change for this is the change in your mindset.

Get-better summary

1. The philosophy of get-better is about getting better results for the same effort. That purpose is also served by leveraging our external ecosystem better.
2. We must recognize that vendors don't necessarily offer the same quality of service to all their clients. Our simple intention must be: how do we get the best out of them for their current capability? And to be able to do that, we must move our mindset from *a vendor orientation to a partnership orientation.*
3. The quality of people in the ecosystem is crucial and the *right remuneration* can help that. To decide the remuneration, don't look only at direct costs but at the impact of the partner on your business performance.

4. A key aspect of improving the external ecosystem is cultural and is often a function of the tone and *role modelling at a leadership level*.
5. Successful companies and individuals of the future will be those who can make their *external ecosystem a force multiplier* and that requires a mindset shift to start with.

SECTION 4

Getting better is not just about us getting better. It is also about making our ecosystem get better as it serves a common purpose—the purpose of getting greater results for a given effort from us. If we keep getting better but the ecosystem around us does not improve, we'll end up wasting a lot of our effort making up for that weak ecosystem.

Sometimes, we underestimate how much difference a superior ecosystem can make and our efforts towards that. We tend to think that making the team better is something HR needs to be concerned with. We lose sight of what we can do to make a better team. The same thing applies to the external ecosystem as well; we underestimate how much improvement you can bring about if you are determined to make a difference. I want to recount my experience at Onida, where I worked from 2001 to 2005 as VP, sales and marketing.

The beginning of my stint in Onida coincided with the early stages of LG and Samsung in the durables market in India, and those two brands took the market by storm. It was very challenging for an Indian brand to stand up to that competition. BPL, a leading Indian brand, was the market leader at the time, and it folded up in a few years, unable to match the Korean competition. When I joined Onida, it was much smaller than BPL and logically, we should also have folded up. Yet, in four years, we nearly doubled the revenue and made progress on multiple fronts.

What did we do differently? It was in building a superior ecosystem. Between 2001 and 2005, we built one of the best sales and marketing teams in the durables industry. And we created and nurtured a tremendous external partner ecosystem, which multiplied our efforts. Onida did not survive the competition because it had better technology, Onida did not survive because we had deep financial resources and spent money irrationally—it then was one of the most prudent companies when it came to spending money. But we could do what BPL could not do—grow and flourish in that phase of four years. This was possible because we simply made our ecosystem better and focused on making our people better and our external partnerships better. Do not underestimate how much difference a determined effort to make your team and your external ecosystem better can make to your results and performance.

As a consequence of Sections 1–3, you have a full range of techniques you can adopt to get better and improve your GBM significantly. While the get-better techniques can be applied to any situation or context, there are some specific situations that many people have questions about. In Section 4, I tackle the application of the get-better methodology to a specific set of contexts and applications. I will try to answer specific questions like:

1. What do I do if my career has stagnated and I can't get out of the rut?

2. What if I don't have the right education, like an MBA degree; can I make up for it?
3. How do I manage career life cycles?
4. What if I work in a start-up? Do these principles work for me?
5. How do I get better at being more effective in meetings?

Questions like these are answered in the next four chapters.

11

Stagnating Careers and the MBA versus non-MBA Conundrum

After the success of *Catalyst*, many people wrote to me about their career problems. An overwhelming number of them were a variation of 'My career is stagnating. I am trying hard, putting in all the effort I can, but I am not succeeding'. And it was frustrating for those people that despite their best efforts, they were unable to advance their careers, which seemed stuck in a rut. Equally, there are many who have good careers now, but are not aware that their careers could stagnate somewhere down the line. This chapter will help those whose careers are stuck and the same principles will help those doing well to prevent getting stuck in the future.

We have all seen that person who has been doing the same job for many years now, with no career progress. It could be the person in sales handling the same region for a long time, or the person in accounts handling payments ever since you joined, or that person in procurement who has been procuring the same material from the same vendors day after day, or that relationship manager in a bank who has been managing the same relationships without much success. Such examples abound and usually, both the company and the individual have made their peace with the status quo. If you are such a person, how can you free your career from such a situation? If you are the manager to such a person, how can you help that person extricate their career from the logjam it is in now?

The starting point is the self-diagnosis of the problem. I have observed that it's easy to externalize the reasons for not making progress in one's career. The diagnosis can range from office politics, bad luck, 'I don't have a fancy degree', 'I don't have a godfather' to 'I don't know how to make good presentations' and 'only people who are good at presentations win', and on and on it goes. Externalizing this problem is not going to help you further your career. The real reason careers get stuck is because we stop getting better. That is the simple truth, and if you don't accept it, you won't find the key to pushing your career out of the quicksand it is in.

Sometimes, externalizing the problem seems appropriate because you see people who produce similar results make career progress while you don't, and you immediately feel victimized. However, as mentioned in Chapter 2, for advancement, organizations look at both current results and the ability to produce future results. It is possible that in their assessment, while your current results are similar, the other person might have a higher ability to produce future results in new situations because they have a better GBM than yours.

Careers have two stages. I call them the 'time stage' and the 'GBM stage'. The 'time stage' is the early stage of your career, say the first ten years or so. In this stage, even if we don't know the answers, we get them from our bosses and the rest of the organization. There is no pressure on us to discern the method of finding the answers. It is possible to be reasonably successful by implementing those answers well. This gives us some career growth, and this is what I call the 'time stage' of the career. The progression of years and hard work can get you career growth and most people are able to make progress in the time stage of their careers.

The game changes as you become middle management around 10–15 years into your career. Suddenly, work changes from implementing the answers others have given you to having to find the answers yourself. People who can find the answers at this stage are those who have a good GBM. Only such people experience career progress from this stage onwards, and hence I call it the 'GBM stage' of careers.

When I see people with stagnant careers, it feels like they came through the time stage successfully but got stuck at the beginning of the GBM stage and did not make progress after that. Because people experience easy career growth in the time stage, they do not focus adequately on getting better and improving their GBMs. And when they hit the GBM stage, they stagnate because unfortunately, they have not developed the habit of getting better. If you remember, in Chapter 1, I observed that many people taxi and reach the runway, but only some take off and soar. The explanation is in the difference between the time stage and the GBM stage. Everybody gets through the time stage, but only some get to soar in the GBM stage.

A summary of all my observations on careers is:

1. Most people have poor GBMs; as a result they do not get better enough to go beyond the time stage to the GBM stage.
2. Ninety-five out of 100 people experience career growth in the time stage. Only about fifteen out of 100 experience career growth in the GBM stage.*

This problem gets further compounded by the pyramids that organizational structures are. Companies need many more people at the lower to middle levels and people in the time stage are suitable for those. Companies need fewer people in the upper half of the pyramid. As a result, they can make do with the few people who have the GBMs to fill those positions. Hence, companies make limited efforts to grow the GBMs of those who have got stuck in the time stage of their careers. Over time, these people get slotted into roles where they have

* I don't have any validated method of proving these numbers. These are just estimates, and it is possible the estimate is wrong. But the core point, that most people succeed in the time stage and very few succeed in the GBM stage, is quite clear in my mind.

a high comfort level and high domain familiarity, and are utilized for the maximum value they can create in the time-stage roles. A vicious cycle begins—they do familiar roles, the same answers work again and again, there is no need to get drastically better and where they don't have answers, somebody else helps them. The sum total of that is that the GBM never develops and the career stagnation is now complete and final. Getting stuck in a role where you have been very comfortable for a long time is one of the clearest signals that you are heading for career stagnation.

The characteristics I see in people who have stagnated are:

1. They have a lot of answers, but lack the method of finding the answers. Hence, they have very low domain independence.
2. They lack the pilot's view, the big-picture capability. They visualize and articulate issues only from their current level without connecting to the macro picture.
3. They lack the ability to build and leverage a high-quality team. Often, their team comprises people like them, people who are successful because they are in the time stage. They are unable to attract and retain people who have a high-quality GBM. This furthers the vicious cycle of not producing breakthrough thinking and results.

Once you have accepted the core issue—that you have to get better, improve your GBM and not externalize the problem—the two steps to reinvigorating your stagnating career are:

1. Prioritize getting better as opposed to only producing results.
2. Start building your GBM afresh.

In Chapter 2, I wrote about the need to *prioritize getting better*, not just producing results. That is particularly important for people with stagnating careers. You have already produced results for a few years and that has not helped your career. Why would one more year of results change that? Don't fall into the trap of thinking—'I will first produce results and if I have time after that, I will focus on getting better'. Change it around—devote 5–10 per cent of your time to getting better, even if it feels like it is at the cost of results.

To *build the GBM afresh* you have to force yourself to get out of comfortable situations and into situations where you don't have the answers and the capabilities required. There are two ways of doing that:

1. Take up a new role in a new domain where you don't know the answers. You will be forced to get to the methods of finding the answers and to build new capabilities. There is, of course, some risk involved in this, but if the risk is manageable, I do strongly advocate domain change as a way of unlocking stuck careers. The first role in the new domain might not give you immediate career benefits as your performance in that

role will be moderate, because you are still building the GBM. The first role will unlock the process of rebuilding the stagnant GBM; the career benefits will be in future roles.

2. If you can't get a new role or don't want to take the risk, find a way of dealing with new situations even in your current role. Try and solve the more complex issues that you have been skirting so far. Try and volunteer for special projects in a different field in your company even if there is no career benefit. And when you get nominated to such project teams, go out of your way to make a difference and contribute; don't stay within your comfort level. I have often nominated loyal, committed managers in the company to project teams to help them get better. It is frustrating when they don't get out of their comfort zone to make a contribution and remain passengers in such teams. When you get an opportunity, make the most of it.

MBA versus non-MBA

The other barrage of questions I have faced has been from non-MBAs who feel frustrated that their careers don't progress as much as those of the MBAs. I am using MBA versus non-MBA to exemplify the situation of having, or not having, a fancy degree. I have heard disgruntled BCom students who feel that CAs get an unfair advantage, diploma holders who feel engineers get an unfair advantage, and even, for that matter, Tier-3

MBAs who feel Tier-1 MBAs get an unfair advantage. So when I deal with an MBA versus a non-MBA situation, the solutions and the principles apply to all such situations.

The first thing to do is to address the psychological aspect, i.e. not have a victim mindset. Stop thinking that it is unfair that the MBA gets an advantage over you—that is not going to solve your problem. The world is not going to change overnight; you have to change if you want to succeed. The beginning of that change is to stop blaming the world for your problems.

I was conducting a session in a company once and was asked a question by one such person, who felt that not doing an MBA had put her at a disadvantage, which she felt was unfair. It was clear from the tone of her question that she believed that those who gained by doing an MBA did not really deserve it, and the degree provided an unfair advantage. I asked her about her educational qualifications and she told me she had graduated with a BSc in Maths. I then asked her a question: There are many people who finish high school but don't go to college after that. The highest qualification they have is twelfth grade at high school. I asked her, should she have an advantage over such people because she has done a BSc? She fumbled, but the question hit home. She understood that she wanted to retain the advantage her BSc gave her over those who have just done twelfth grade, but she felt it was unfair if an MBA got an advantage over her. If you don't want an MBA to have an advantage over a non-MBA, you should be comfortable losing the advantage of your education to an uneducated person; it has to cut the same way in both situations. Hence, the starting point to resolving this is to stop thinking of yourself as a victim, stop thinking of fairness and unfairness, and start to think about what you can do to get better to improve your career. Sorry for the strong words—I am an MBA myself and hence, you might feel that it is easy for me to say this. But if I don't get you to change your thinking, you will not make progress, and my strong words have only that intent.

I observed this phenomenon closely, having worked in companies which had both MBAs and non-MBAs, to try and understand if there is a genuine difference in the individuals that explains the difference in career trajectories, or is it just the credentials of the fancy degree that provide the career advantage. One place where you get to compare both people side-by-side is in sales, where you often have the equivalent of area sales managers of both MBA and non-MBA types in the same organization. The MBAs often become ASMs straight after training, while the non-MBAs usually work for a few years as frontline salespersons before they become area managers. As I observed these two groups, I saw a clear pattern:

1. I observed that in the first year of the role, the non-MBA often performed much better than the MBA in a similar role.

2. I observed that in the second year of the same role, the non-MBA did not show a significant improvement in performance compared to the first year, but there was a remarkable improvement in the performance of the MBA; they often outperformed the non-MBA.

This told me a few things, which are very important to understand:

1. The non-MBA had high familiarity with the domain, having come up the ranks. In the first year, they performed better because they already had many of the answers. The MBA had zero domain familiarity in the early stages and no ready-made answers, and hence, they struggled initially.
2. The MBA, however, had a GBM that allowed them to learn rapidly and get better to a remarkable extent in their first year, which improved their performance in the second year. The non-MBA lacked the GBM, and hence, they performed similarly in their second year. Their answers to the situations remained the same. They did not evolve.

As a result, I concluded that the difference in careers was because the MBAs seemed to have a better GBM, got better faster and their ability to learn was higher. The benefit of the education is not the rubber stamp of the degree, but the learning ability, the GBM, it creates.

The other thing that gives MBAs an advantage over the non-MBAs is the way organizations stereotype. This stereotyping has two distinct results:

1. MBAs often get the more complex, challenging roles, which allow them to get better at an even more rapid pace.
2. Senior managers in the organization often have a different approach to managing the two groups of people. I find that senior managers primarily focus on relationship-building with non-MBAs, investing in getting to know them better and building a personal relationship to cultivate loyalty. With MBAs, I find that senior managers often focus on coaching and helping the MBA get better, teaching and developing them.

Now, some of this stereotyping is justified as there is a difference in the GBM quality. The organizational stereotyping is only a response to its accumulated experience of dealing with these two groups. I recognize that some of the stereotyping and consequent actions might actually be the root cause of the GBM difference. It is difficult to say which is the chicken and which is the egg, but to some extent, they are both true.

Most times, the response of a non-MBA to a stuck career is to say, let me also do an MBA and get the rubber stamp of the degree. Many pursue evening MBA or postal MBA, and some even take a few years' break from work to do a full-time MBA. After that, they are often disappointed because it seems to make no difference to their career.

That is because there is a distinct difference in quality between the good B-schools and the average B-schools. The good MBA schools go beyond the curriculum to actually help develop a student's GBM. While the average MBA school does impart textbook knowledge, it does very little to improve the GBM and the learning ability of the student. And as I mentioned above, the career advantage of an MBA is not the rubber stamped degree, but the superior GBM the education helped them build. Unless you do an MBA from a quality institute that goes beyond giving you a degree to building the GBM, it will not work. You will only be wasting your time and your money if it does not change your GBM.

Hence, as a non-MBA, the problem you have to solve is not the absence of the degree, but the possible absence of a GBM. You have to focus on improving your ability to learn, your GBM. If you do that, in a very short time, your career will advance and you will find that there is no difference between you and the MBA. *If your GBM is as good as the MBA's, your career will be as good as the MBA's, even without the degree.*

I have seen this play out all around me. I have seen some remarkable people who started as frontline salesmen without an MBA rise all the way to becoming managing directors in the same company. And having been involved in some of their careers, I found that in any talent discussion session among senior management, seldom did the conversation ever go to their lack of an MBA degree. It was not a criterion in decision-making. The fact that they had built a GBM as good as or better than the MBAs' made the degree irrelevant, and that is how I want you to think. Improve the pace at which you get better, improve your GBM, and you will make the absence of the degree irrelevant to your career.

The principles to get better and improve the GBM are already outlined in the book and I won't repeat them here. But I do want to say the following:

1. The initiative to get better has to come clearly from the non-MBA themselves. That is because as mentioned earlier, sometimes, because of organizational stereotyping, the focus of senior managers and HR on this group is limited.
2. In some cases, it is about challenging yourselves to solve complex problems and operating at a level higher than your normal one. Push yourself to be uncomfortable, that will be the start of the growth journey.
3. Get a mentor who will help you get better. Non-MBAs often end up with benefactors, not mentors. You don't want somebody who will 'take care' of you; you want somebody who will make you better.

The final recommendation I have is to stay the course and not to give up easily. Also, try and have long stints in companies when you are performing well. You are trying to break a stereotype and get a breakthrough promotion, which is normally not available to non-MBAs. Companies and senior managers who know you well are more likely to take such a risk if they know you well. So try and invest a bit of time in the company if possible. Of course, do not be foolish in your loyalty.

There is a saying that when it comes to careers, 'your attitude determines your altitude'. It is even truer in the two situations described above—reinvigorating stuck careers and non-MBA versus MBA. The longer you stick to blaming everybody else and the world, the less progress you will make. As your attitude changes and you focus on what you have to do to change yourself and get better, you will break free of all shackles. One of the inspirations for me in writing this book is the urge to help these two groups of people break free from their shackles. Go forth, focus on changing yourself, embark on a get-better journey and realize all your dreams and ambitions.

Get-better summary

1. To reinvigorate stagnant careers, you have to change the diagnosis from blaming external circumstances to recognizing that you have stopped getting better. That is the root problem you have to solve.
2. There are two stages to careers, the 'time stage' and the 'GBM stage'. Most people who get stuck in their careers get stuck at the end of the time stage and do not manage to succeed in the GBM stage. Ninety-five out of 100 experience career growth in the time stage, but only fifteen out of 100 succeed in the GBM stage.
3. The two steps to reinvigorating a stagnating career are:
    a. Prioritize getting better as opposed to only producing results.

   b. Start building your GBM afresh. A good way to do this is to get to a new domain where you will be forced to find new answers.
4. As a non-MBA, there is nothing gained by thinking the world is unfair in rewarding MBAs. The answer lies in you developing the GBM of an MBA, the degree will then become irrelevant.
5. The real difference between a good MBA and a non-MBA is not in the knowledge they have, but in the GBM and learning ability they have. Hence, getting the stamp of a degree without changing your GBM will not help improve your career.
6. Instead, focus on developing your GBM, for which the initiative has to come from you. Build a relationship with a mentor and try and stick around in companies where you do well to make it easier for people to take a risk and bet on you.

12

Managing Career Life Cycles

The life cycle of a career has two distinct stages. For example, you could be a skilled software professional who has worked for a long time in a pedigreed IT company. You have just joined a new IT company in a similar role. In one week, you get on top of your job and you feel you can do it easily. The key thing that you need to understand is that while the job is familiar, your stage in the career life cycle is different. In your previous company, you had established yourself while in this company, you are still at the infancy stage. So while the content of the job feels similar, it does not mean you can function the same way. Based on where you are in your career life cycle, you have to alter what you do, what you don't do by yourself and where you leverage others. Managing career life cycles is a key area that we need to get better at for long-term success.

The two stages of the career life cycle

1. Early stage: Where you are in the beginning of a new role or in a new company.
2. Mature stage: Where you have spent adequate time in a role or in the same company.

While there are many other subtle nuances to a career life cycle, let us focus on these two stages and understand how to get better at being effective in them.

We want to be successful in our careers, in each role and each company we work in. Success happens when you manage to drive significant positive change in your tenure in a role/company. When you finish a role you should have left it at a much better place than when you started by driving positive change. Nobody becomes successful by preserving status quo. If you leave a role in the same position where it was when you started it, you won't be successful.

To be able to drive that positive change we need to get better in our abilities to drive change. There are two important abilities required for this. First, the ability to spot where change is required or the ability to identify the areas where change is required. The second is the ability to execute the change, which means making the change happen in a successful manner and making the change stick.

The interesting thing is that these abilities are not constant—they are highly influenced by which stage in the career life cycle you are at. Your other abilities, for the most part, don't fluctuate based on the career life cycle—e.g., your analytical ability is unlikely to fluctuate when you go from a mature stage in a previous company to an early stage in a new company. However, your ability to spot and execute change fluctuates significantly based on your career life cycle stage. Hence, to be successful, it is important to not only drive positive change but also get better at understanding how your change abilities operate at different career stages.

As stated above, there are two change abilities:

1. Ability to spot the opportunities to drive positive change, hereafter referred to as the *ability to spot change*.
2. Ability to execute change, make the change happen and stick, hereafter referred to as the *ability to execute change*.

The diagram below will help us understand how these two abilities fluctuate in the career life cycle:

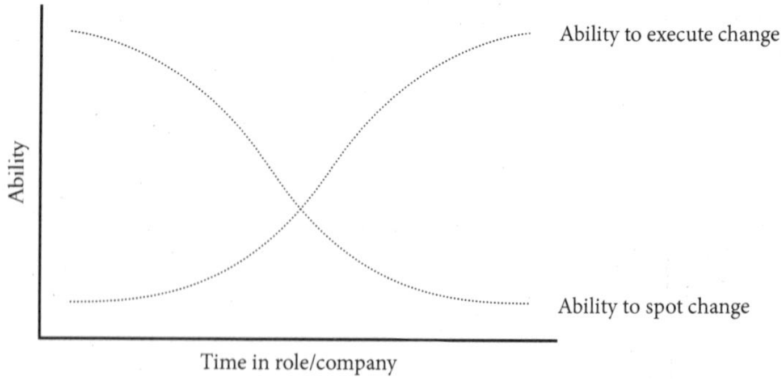

The x-axis of the diagram is the time you have spent in a role/company. It is a marker of the career life cycle stage. The more left you are, the earlier the stage you are at, and the more right you are, the more mature the stage you are at. The y-axis of the diagram is the extent of the change abilities you have. As you can see, there are two curves there, the curve of the ability to spot change and the curve of the ability to execute change. At the simplest level, what you can see is that your ability to spot change is at its highest at an early stage and diminishes as you hit the mature stage, and vice versa for your ability to execute change, which is at its lowest at an early stage, grows continuously and is at its highest at the mature stage.

Ability to spot change

The ability to spot change is at its highest in the early stage because of the following reasons:

1. You are able to see the big picture easily without getting lost in the details.
2. You have fresh eyes and you are not immersed in any of the current activities and programmes. Hence, you are not defensive, not trying to justify anything and, as a result, you can see a spade as a spade.

The exact opposite of these reasons is why your ability to spot change diminishes to its lowest at the mature stage. You get lost in the details, you are solving level-two, level-three problems and you lose your big-picture lens. For example, in a new role I could spot that the primary problem is that the market itself is underdeveloped and we have to develop the market. But with the passing of time, a lot of my attention starts going to level-two, level-three problems. For example, I might notice that X city is not growing—how do I fix that? Or the packaging vendor has a problem—how do I get a new vendor? So much of my attention and energy gets consumed by these level-two and three problems that I no longer focus on the level-one problem of developing the market.

Also, many of the programmes and activities in the mature stage are things you probably initiated and drove and hence, you are deeply invested in them, almost to the point of defensiveness. Hence, you are unable to see the need for change in them.

Ability to execute change

The ability to execute change is at its lowest in the early stages because:

1. To execute change, you must have a good understanding of the organization, its culture and its stakeholders. This is poor in the early stage.
2. Driving change requires credibility for others to agree and follow you. While you might have high capability even at an early stage because of your experience, your credibility is built in a new role/company only over time. Your credibility is low in the early stages and not enough to drive big change. Do not confuse capability with credibility.
3. Lastly, executing change requires reasonably good personal relationships with all key entities who will enable the change and participate in it. These relationships are inadequately developed in the early stage.

As time passes, these aspects start to change and your ability to execute change improves. Your understanding of stakeholders, organizational culture and key influencers gets better. Your personal credibility starts to grow and people are willing to follow you in a journey of change, and lastly, your relationships grow to be able to manage the change. Hence, your ability to execute change is at its highest in a mature stage.

The challenge is that the two abilities required, the ability to spot change and the ability to execute change, are never high at the same time. So whenever you try to drive change, you are weak in one of the two abilities. This is the reason most people fail to drive big change and that impacts their career success.

The answer to this challenge lies in getting better in two areas:

1. Getting better at *leveraging the strengths* when they are high, i.e. how to leverage the strength of your ability to spot change in the early stages and ability to execute it at more mature stages.
2. Getting better at *leveraging others in the weakness areas*, i.e. how to leverage others to execute change in the early stages and how to leverage others to spot change in the mature stages.

Early stage

The early stage is when you have just entered a new role or a new company. At this stage, your strength is your ability to spot the change opportunity and your weakness is the ability to execute the change. Let us apply the above two principles to determine what you should do in the early stage.

Leverage the strength of your ability to spot the change opportunity. I have personally practised two ways of doing this. The first is that I make a note at the end of ninety days about what I seek to accomplish in the next three years. In the first ninety days, my vision is still fresh. I can ask many questions and understand the situation as it really is. I don't know enough of the details to lose my way. I can see the big picture and can quite easily see the important things that need to be done. This note I write on a piece of paper, often no longer than one page. In a way, this is a note to myself on what change I want to drive in my three-year tenure in that role. In fact, when I joined Cadbury, I wrote this note to myself on what change I would accomplish at a very early stage, and that note, handwritten in 2005, is still with me.

The second way I do it is to embark on a strategy creation exercise very early on in my role, before I get too deep into operations. I typically create this strategy in the first 3–4 months of being in the role, and that serves as my lodestar for what I want to do in the next three years. I practised this when I took on HR in Cadbury, a field I had no idea of as I was largely a sales and marketing person before that. I practised this when I joined Pidilite and created the strategy for the Dr Fixit waterproofing business very early in my time there. In both these situations, I went through a full strategy creation exercise with my team in the first few months of my time there.

Leverage others in the weakness area of ability to execute change. I typically advise people not to execute a big change in the early stage because the probability of such change succeeding is low. However, there are some situations in your career where it is important to execute change even in the early stages. If you are in such a situation, it still does not change the reality that your ability to execute change is low at that point. The need to execute the change does not change the ability to do so. You have to recognize that and not be foolhardy in trying to execute the change by yourself. This is the time to get better at leveraging others; identify members of your team who are at a mature stage and have the ability to execute and drive the change on your behalf. Your boss could also be a person you leverage to drive the change on your behalf. It is important to get better at leveraging others to drive the change in the early stages.

Changing the team at an early stage

Sometimes, when people join a new role/company, the first thing they do is make wholesale changes in their team. They replace many of the existing team members with new employees and shuffle many people. Using our framework, let us examine if this is sensible. As we agreed, what is weak in the early stages is the ability to execute, and when we make sweeping changes in the team, we only compound our weakness further. When we bring many new people in, in effect, what we are doing is adding to the ability to spot, which is already a strength for you, and weakening further the ability to execute, which is already a weakness. I strongly advise against doing such a thing. When I have a joined a new place, seldom have I made major people changes in the first few months. I always try and work with the people who are already there as they make up for my weakness, which is the ability to execute, in the early stages.

Building the pipe

The other important thing to get better at in the early stages is to build relationships with others in the organization and stakeholders outside the organization. Imagine an oilfield that has a lot of oil. A person digs the oilfield, but when the oil starts gushing out, they realize that they have forgotten to build the pipes to carry that oil. All the oil is then wasted. The content of change is the oil, and the relationships with people and stakeholders are the pipelines to carry the oil. If you focus only on building the change content, like the strategy and the one-pager note I described above, but don't also build the pipeline called relationships to carry that change content, you won't be successful. So in the early stage of your career life cycle, you have to do two things—build the change content, leveraging your ability to spot change, and in parallel, build the relationships, the pipeline to carry out that change later.

There is a simple way I recommend to build relationships. When you join a new place, start by listing who all you want to build a relationship with. Then I recommend you organize what I call 'no agenda' meetings. It is possible by then that you have figured out what you want from them, which key change areas you want to push, but I still want you to have the first meeting without any requirements from your side. Instead, I want you to do two things in the first meeting with that person. One is to understand what they do, and two, ask them, 'What can I do to help you?' From the list of things they give you, wherever you can help them, try and get one or two things done and go and meet them again. If you do this in the first 3–4 months, you will see an extraordinary building of relationship pipes which can carry the oil that you want to pump through later. One of the biggest mistakes I have made is rushing in with my agenda early on without building relationships. This is like digging for oil without taking the time to build the pipe. Sometimes, when you lay a pipe, you feel there is no value being created because nothing is going through it. And in that anxiety, you dig for oil too fast without having the patience to lay the pipes. Relationship-building is essential in the early stage; if you have the pipes, you can pump the oil of change through it at a later stage, but if you don't have the pipes, nothing can be pumped through them.

Mature stage

The mature stage is when you have spent a fair amount of time in your role/company. In the mature stage, your ability to execute the change is very high and is your strength, but your ability to spot the change is reduced and is a weakness.

This is the time to leverage your strength and execute big change. In this phase, if you stick to the status quo, you have missed the opportunity to make a difference and it will impact your long-term success. The important thing in executing the change is to stay true to the one-pager strategy you created at the early stage, when your ability to spot the change was high. Many people get into the trap of making new strategies and change agendas, which often lacks the big-picture quality of the first change agenda you made. As I mentioned earlier, I made a one-pager for myself when I joined Cadbury in 2005. One of the change agendas I had written for myself then was to bring Cadbury into the post-dinner sweet segment. It took me till 2011 to execute the agenda as, till then, I could not get the influence and the opportunity to execute it. But when I got the opportunity in 2011, instead of creating a new agenda, I executed what I had written on a piece of paper in 2005 and created a memorable advertising campaign called '*Khaane ke baad, kuch meetha ho jaye*', which means 'let us have something sweet after dinner'. This discipline, to stay true to the original big picture thinking and then use the enhanced ability to execute those big picture changes, is crucial in the maturity stage.

Leveraging others to overcome one's weakness in the ability to spot change is crucial in this phase. The best way to do this is to talk to people who are new and have the enhanced ability to spot change. I have often practised sitting with new people and asking them a simple question, 'If you were doing my job, what is the one thing you would do that I am not doing today?' This would quickly get me to what new people see as the burning need for change, and would often take me back to the big picture from the details I got lost in during the mature stage. I have seen senior people get such suggestions, but do nothing about them because they have heard them before and have lived with those problems for a long time. Just because you have lived with a problem does not mean it is not a problem. For instance, when a new person comes to a particularly dirty city, they will immediately spot the need for change in cleanliness. However, it is possible that the leaders of the city have heard of this problem 1000 times because they are in a mature stage and hence, do not spot the desperate need for change there. The single biggest problem in the ability to spot change at the mature stage is that we simply can't spot the most obvious problems to solve and drive change in. We keep looking for less obvious and more complex problems to drive the change in, and end up wasting our strength in the ability to execute by not attacking the big, bold issues.

The other way to leverage others to overcome the weakness in our ability to spot change is to bring new blood into the team. While in the initial stages, I recommend minimal changes to the team, at the mature stage, it is important to drive calibrated change in the team to improve the ability to spot change. I do not, however, want this to be interpreted as a licence to be irresponsible with people's careers. Irrespective of the changes we want to drive, we must be responsible with people who are currently in those roles. I was once in a very high-performing leadership team and my boss, Anand Kripalu, a truly outstanding leader, had this simple model of changing one member of the leadership team every year in a calibrated way. The team functioned outstandingly well because we always had enough people with both the strengths—ability to spot and ability to execute. Never end up with a team where everybody has the same strength and the same weakness. Another good way to improve the ability to spot change, especially for senior managers, is to attend high-quality training programmes that can be the stimulus to big-picture thinking again.

A challenge in the mature stage is that the things that need to change are things that you have personally been involved in and have deep vested interests in. Hence, even when you hear from newer people that this needs to change, there is a tendency to rationalize it. It comes from a sense of insecurity—if I change this, I am actually accepting that what I did was wrong. That notion stops us from accepting what others spotted as a need for change. Everything has a time and a place—what you did might have been the right thing to do when you did it, but you don't have to protect it forever and become a prisoner of your past. When others spot the need for change and you hear it again and again from them, agree to explore the change even if what currently exists was your creation.

Acquisitions

Mergers and acquisitions are a routine part of the corporate landscape nowadays. There is overwhelming research to suggest that most acquisitions do not create long-term value. I don't want to begin that debate here; that is for a strategy book to cover. But I do want to talk about why acquisitions fail, using the ability to spot and ability to execute frameworks.

When a company acquires another, the senior managers of the acquiring company enter the early stage of the career life cycle again. They have a very high ability to spot what change is required in the acquired company, and they are often right about the change needs they spot. But they don't realize that their ability to execute the change is very low. Another thing that happens in acquisitions, which further weakens the ability to execute change, is that many of the senior management of the acquired company are either forced to leave or leave of their own volition. Not only are the managers of the acquiring company in the early stage, weak in their ability to execute change, but they also lose the execution strength in the acquired company because of the exit of the other leaders. So in sum, the ability to execute change is abysmally low in the early stage of an acquisition. However, in the urge to show positive results from the acquisition, the acquiring company often pushes through an agenda of big change despite a poor ability to execute it. That creates a complete mess and destroys any long-term value from the acquisition.

To make acquisitions work for the long-term, there are two simple models:

1. If you want to make big change, make the big change leveraging the managers of the acquired company. Do not drive big change in management teams and people in the acquired company in this situation.

2. Alternatively, if there are big changes in management teams, postpone big change till the ability to execute change is strengthened again. A large number of people with high ability to spot change and low ability to execute change are the perfect recipe for disaster if you drive big change.

I do want to add a disclaimer here that my analysis of acquisitions is only from the limited perspective of the change framework I have developed. The success and failure of acquisitions depend on many things, including strategic fit, price and value, synergies, etc., and I don't want to suggest that my framework is the only driver of success.

Get-better summary

1. There are two distinct career life cycle stages—the early stage, when you are new in a role/company, and the mature stage, when you have spent enough time in a role/company.
2. To be successful, you have to drive positive change; maintaining status quo does not create success. To drive positive change, you need:
   a. The ability to spot change.
   b. The ability to execute the change.
3. At early stages, the ability to spot is high and the ability to execute is low, and vice versa for the mature stage. The key challenge is that both the change abilities are never high at the same time.

4. To overcome that challenge, it is important that at each stage, you get better at leveraging the strength you have and get better at leveraging others to overcome the weakness you have.
5. Early stage
    a. Leverage your strength in the ability to spot by writing down a ninety-day note on the next three-year plan or by doing a full strategy exercise early.
    b. Overcome weakness in execution by leveraging your boss or your team members to execute change.
6. Mature stage
    a. Leverage your strength in the ability to execute by driving big change. It is important to go back to the change opportunities you spotted at your early stage for execution now rather than creating new ones which might lack the big picture quality.
    b. Overcome weakness in your ability to spot change by asking new people and being very open to what they are saying.

13

Getting Better at Meetings

Anybody who has a job ends up being a part of many official meetings. Meetings consume a lot of time and a fair amount of energy. Most people I have met complain about meetings, how they take up too much time, how they are not productive and little of consequence gets done and so on. The interesting thing is this complaint comes from both entities, the leaders of the meetings as well as the participants of the meetings. It is clear that we need to get more effective at meetings to better manage our time and productivity at work.

An effective meeting must result in the following:

1. The results must improve because of that meeting being held.
2. People who attend the meeting must get better.

Most meetings primarily tend to focus on the first point; there is quite a limited focus on the second one. I believe people will be much more enthusiastic about meetings if they got better as a result of attending meetings. The interesting thing is that most meetings underemphasize getting better because they want to focus on better results, but in reality meetings don't do a good job of even improving the results. In this chapter I would like to introduce a framework for effective meetings which gets us to both the outcomes—improved results as well as getting better in meetings.

To improve the results, it is important to have a simple framework for producing results. The simplest framework I use has these three components:

1. We know which outcomes/results we are chasing.
2. We know what the most important drivers for those results are.
3. We know how to influence those drivers positively to impact the end result.

I want to introduce a simple framework which I call the 'result-drivers' framework or

> the Y = f(X) framework, where Y is the result and the Xs are the drivers.

For example, if the outcome we are interested in is related to costs in a factory, the result and the drivers would look like this:

> Outcome (Y): Total cost in the factory
> Drivers (Xs): Raw material cost, packaging cost, employees' cost, wastage and yield, utility costs

like electricity or steam, overhead costs like canteen, administration, transport, etc.
Each of these is a separate driver and can be denoted as X1, X2 and so on.

In this framework, as we think about improving the result (Y), the method of finding the answer is twofold:

1. Identifying all the drivers (Xs) which impact that result
2. Improving those drivers which make the greatest difference.

You start improving the results only if you continuously get better at both these steps and effective meetings are a crucial stepping-stone to this.

The right framework for meetings

The starting point to effective meetings is to be very clear on which results (Ys) the meeting is aimed at. Often there are meetings where the participants do not have a shared understanding of which Ys they are trying to work on. Different participants come into the meeting with different Ys which they want to improve and what ensues is what we colloquially call a *khichdi*, a complete mishmash of a meeting. In the factory cost meeting, if the finance person wants to improve the cost, but the production person wants to improve the volume produced and the HR person in the same meeting wants to decrease attrition, no progress will be made. It is important to get the entire group aligned to solving the same 'Y'. Different people can have different ways of solving it—that is fine—but if different people start solving for different Ys then it becomes a completely non-productive meeting. If there are different Ys that have to be solved, then ideally each Y should be solved in a different meeting, not the same meeting. Meetings are most productive when all participants work towards the same outcome.

The second step is to define Y = f(X). A clear listing of all the drivers that can impact Y has to be prepared in advance and all the participants should be aware of the drivers and be in agreement.

Once the results and the drivers are defined, the actual meeting should proceed as follows:

1. First discuss the outcome itself—have the results improved, remained the same or worsened? What are the short-term and long-term trends of Y?
2. Then review the drivers, all the Xs. Here, it is necessary to review the drivers in order of importance, with the most important driver first and the least important driver last.
3. Most importantly, improve your understanding of the relationship between outcome and drivers. When the Y and Xs are discussed in the same meeting the participants will be able to understand the linkages. They are able to draw inferences on which X impacts Y and by how much.

4. Make a plan for how you will improve the Xs to achieve Y.

This above framework may seem simple, but it is seldom practised. I want to highlight some of the common mistakes I see in meetings everywhere.

Discussing drivers without understanding the outcome

A mistake I often find is that instead of discussing the outcome first and understanding the change there, people go straight to reviewing the drivers. That prevents you from understanding the relationship between the outcome and the drivers. In such situations, the driver discussion becomes what I call a 'meaningless activity review', which is discussing something without knowing why it was done in the first place. The purpose of the driver is to impact the outcome. They should never be reviewed without starting with the outcome.

For example, I have seen meetings in HR on the annual appraisal process which discuss only the drivers—how many appraisal forms were filled on time, has the superior signed off in the IT system, etc. These are the drivers. If you don't start with the desired outcome of the annual appraisal process, which is not about just getting forms filled, you will not make meaningful progress.

Reviewing unimportant drivers before the important ones

The second mistake I often see in meetings is that instead of reviewing drivers in order of importance, the less important drivers get discussed first, leaving no time for the more important ones. Let us say that a meeting of one hour is spent discussing a ten-slide PowerPoint deck. On slide two is a point that triggers a long discussion, which consumes all the time, and the meeting ends. In reality, there were very important drivers in slides six and nine that did not even come up for discussion and the entire time was spent on possibly a less important driver in slide two. The simplest solution I found to this problem, which I practise all the time, is to process all ten slides first before the discussion starts. I request everybody else in the meeting to keep quiet till all the ten slides are done. This ensures that the discussion moves straightaway to the most important drivers, even if they were on the last slide and not the first. Seeing the picture as a whole first, understanding which drivers have the biggest impact on the result and then spending time improving those drivers is crucial to more effective meetings.

In my own life, the transition from sales and marketing to HR taught me a lot about results and drivers. I found that in sales and marketing, when you want to improve an outcome, there are often just one or two drivers you focus on and they start to change the outcome. The result–driver relationships are a lot more linear and a lot less complex. When I came to HR, I found that it was much more complex. Firstly, there was little clarity on which results we were chasing—the HR function primarily chases activities. The second problem I identified was that the most important results had very complex drivers, with no simple linear solutions. For instance, employee attrition is a major result area for the

HR function, and I was quite keen, like all HR heads, to try and reduce the attrition in my company. However, I found that the outcome of attrition had many drivers, like the level of people engagement, compensation, the quality of company leadership, the quality of line managers, career growth prospects, industry demand and supply of talent, etc. Because it is so complex, there is a tendency to not construct the Y = f(X) framework. And then what happens? Meetings on attrition tend to focus on idea generation. Somebody will suggest, 'Let us have fun Friday evenings to reduce attrition,' and so an activity gets created. Future review meetings will assess how 'fun Friday evenings' are going and by then, everybody has lost sight of why they are being held in the first place.

However difficult it was, I still did the following:

1. Understood all the results I was trying to improve. Mindless activity without knowing which result areas you are improving is the greatest waste of time and resources.
2. Understood which drivers will improve the results. However complex this might be, if you don't construct a Y = f(X) model and understand all the Xs, there is a lowered chance you will actually improve the Y.
3. Understood the Xs in order of importance. You must know whether it is compensation or people engagement that is more important at this point of time to reduce attrition. All drivers are not equally important.

4. Focused on improving the most important Xs. Activity done to improve the most important drivers is useful activity, not meaningless activity.
5. Never had a meeting to review just the activity. Every meeting would review the result and the drivers holistically.

I would like each of you to do the following for the next few minutes. Write down the most important result areas you want to improve at work. These must be the result areas (Ys) and not the drivers (Xs):

....

....

....

Now analyse which meetings discuss these result areas and make a plan to change each of those to a result–driver framework meeting. Do this one thing and you will be amazed at the improvement in both your capabilities and your results.

Implementing the Y = f(X) framework for meetings and conducting it the way I have recommended above will have the twin impact of improving your results as well as significantly improving your methods of finding the answers. In complex situations, answers are not simple and not just about one X. The more you use the framework, the better your method of finding the answers to situations with multiple Xs will be.

Apart from the framework, I have a few other tips on how to use meetings to get better.

Get better by yourself

As discussed in Chapter 6, meetings where people senior to you are present is a great opportunity to build a pilot's view. Please refer to that chapter for more details.

Get better by leveraging others

Meetings are a great opportunity to leverage others for you to get better. As a junior participant I have often asked many questions in meetings which have helped me understand things better and build my capabilities.

For example, there would be meetings in every company where seniors present the plans of the next year to juniors. Many times these presentations tend to state the plans as conclusions reached without explaining how it was arrived at. This is effectively somebody presenting an answer without explaining the method by which they found it. In such meetings I have often asked the questions 'Why? and 'How did we reach this conclusion?' to help me understand the method by which that plan was reached.

Sometimes people hesitate to ask such questions because they think it will waste time. Or they might be worried of what the senior people in the meeting will think. Do not hesitate to ask questions. As a senior I have always wanted people to ask such questions because I know that people who truly understand the plan will do a much better job at execution. Seniors welcome such questions as long as the intent is, 'I want to understand it better so that I can do a good job of implementing it.'

Get-better summary

1. Meetings are often not productive and do not do enough to improve the result as well as help the participants get better.
2. The results–driver framework for Y = f(X), if implemented well in meetings, can have a transformational impact:
    a. It will improve your method of finding the answers to complex situations.
    b. It will help improve your results.
3. The steps to implementing the Y = f(x) framework are:
    a. Define which Y is being addressed in the meeting. Ideally one meeting must address only one Y and all participants must be aligned to that.
    b. Define all the Xs that impact that Y.
    c. Review the Y first in the meeting.
    d. Then review all the Xs ideally in the order of importance.
    e. Make plans to impact the Xs so as to improve the Y.

4. Frequent errors that happen should be avoided:
    a. Conducting meetings where different participants are focused on different Ys.
    b. Participants don't have a shared understanding of the Y = f(X). They don't know all the drivers that impact the Y and it is not defined in advance.
    c. Reviewing drivers and activity without starting at the result.
    d. Reviewing unimportant drivers first and not spending adequate time on the important ones.
5. Meetings are also a great platform to help you get better at developing the pilot's view and to ask questions to understand things.

14

Start-Ups, Professionals and Education

The start-up ecosystem is an important part of our business landscape and many of you may be involved in, or have friends who are part of, start-ups. You might think that a lot of the get-better principles I articulate in this book are not applicable in an entrepreneurial environment. People often say start-ups are too volatile, there is rapid change, it is a VUCA world, etc., to explain why these principles don't work in that environment. Nothing could be further from the truth. Getting better is not an indulgence—something you practise if you have the time and the space afforded by a mature business and a stable job.

This misconception gets magnified due to my background, which people associate more with conventional companies, hence the assumption that these principles I advocate are aimed more at people in traditional, legacy companies.

I'd like to reiterate that these principles are applicable to everybody—people in mature organizations, people in start-ups, professionals like doctors and lawyers practising by themselves, and others. I have thought deeply about the applicability of these principles in all environments. I have also specifically engaged with people with a deep understanding of the start-up ecosystem and its professionals to further validate these principles and sharpen their applications. While the principles are universal, there are some nuances to getting better at start-ups and as professionals and I want to explain that. I also think these nuances are valuable learnings for people in conventional companies as well.

Let me explain why the get-better approach is crucial even in the start-up environment. The success of the start-up is linked intrinsically to the 'getting better' of key people. If those key people don't keep getting better, the start-up will fail. From an employee lens, there is a lot of uncertainty associated with start-ups, and getting better is the only insurance you have for a good future. Hence, getting better is vital for both the start-up company and the people working in the start-up. Explained below are these viewpoints.

The start-up company view

The primary objective of a start-up is survival, followed by scaling up. If you look at both of those, the fundamental progress required is about getting better. A start-up that gets better rapidly is going to survive, scale up and flourish, and a start-up that does not get better rapidly will perish soon. The core truth is that every start-up begins with wanting to solve a problem for the customer, and how much better it gets at solving that problem will determine its future. Hence, getting better is the primary objective of a start-up, not an indulgence.

Most start-ups have an MBP (minimum basic product) that they put into the market and with which they enter a rapid testing and learning curve. Sometimes, the process of continuous product improvement is called sprints—you improve a product, test it, improve it further, test it again and keep sprinting. The core journey of a start-up is a get-better journey and it is important to recognize and internalize that. The interesting thing is that in a start-up, the 'getting better' of the company is intrinsically linked to the 'getting better' of the founders and a few key people. Hence, the survival and the scalability of the company are inextricably linked to the extent to which the founders and key employees get better on a continuous basis.

The start-up is different from a mature business to the extent that in a mature business, getting better rapidly is not such a desperate need. Also, the getting better of the company is not linked to just a few people getting better.

While the need for getting better is clear from the above paragraphs, there are some barriers to that in start-ups. The single biggest barrier is the lack of time and mental space to invest in getting better. The atmosphere is high-pressure and results-oriented and frenetic activity is the norm and, in the process, people keep chasing their tails. I have not been in a start-up, but if I ever am, I am clear that I would put aside at least

5–10 per cent more time and a degree of mental space to get better. The benefits of my getting better to the start-up are much greater than the activity I missed in that 5–10 per cent of working time. I would encourage all start-up founders to embrace this thinking, make getting better a priority for the company and create the time and the space for it.

The second barrier is the orientation of the founders and the key people. Many start-ups are in the technology and digital space and the founders tend to be 'techies'. Not to stereotype, but I do think that the primary orientation of such people is inwards, towards the technology, the product and the applications. As a result, the getting better that is required from a consumer lens is often not given enough attention because the primary comfort zone of the founders is inwards, not outwards. Founders and key people need to be mindful of this and compensate for it using the following techniques:

1. Spend focused time with consumers and applying the principles of review and reflection on that time.
2. Build the right external ecosystem and a diverse team where some people are much more comfortable outwards than inwards. If you build a team that's like you, there is a high risk you will not get better.

Employees' view

If you are an employee in a start-up, especially at the junior or middle level, getting better is crucial to you. Firstly, your getting better increases the probability of the start-up succeeding and hence, it is important. In conventional companies, a junior person getting better does not make a huge difference to the company, but in a start-up it can. Use that opportunity and make a difference to the start-up. The second reason for getting better is to protect your future. Employment in start-ups can be volatile—a start-up can go bust, or reduce headcount for lack of funds. Your only assurance of long-term employability is how much better you have got, and hence, it is mission critical for employees in start-ups to focus on that and not get lost in the frenetic pace and rush of the start-up. When an employee in a conventional company looks for another job, the name and reputation of the company they have worked in helps greatly. Hence, even if a conventional company employee has not got effectively better, they might still get the next job. For a start-up employee, the name and the reputation of the start-up is unlikely to guarantee the next job. Hence, please make sure you are focused on getting better; it is in your interests. Do not postpone it to a future when you think you will be less busy and have more time, because it might be too late then.

Having painted the grim picture, let me also give you the positives. Start-ups offer tremendous opportunities to get better. To leverage that, you must understand some of the nuances:

1. Most start-ups have a lean organization and hence, often have just the founders and many junior people. In effect, it has senior management and junior

management—the middle-management level is underdeveloped as opposed to a mature company. This often creates tremendous space for junior employees as they can take the initiative, occupy the vacant space and do higher order work that will help them get better rapidly. It can expose you to multiple functional domains, strategy conversations and provide opportunities to get better at a higher level. There is massive get-better potential in a start-up; it is just about how much initiative you take.

2. A linked nuance is that developing the pilot's view becomes easier in start-ups, even for junior and middle level employees. In conventional organizations, bosses have more time to coach juniors and that often takes the form of giving answers and directions. In start-ups, there is a lot of self-discovery and that level of active supervision is not available due to thin management teams. Hence, there is the opportunity to operate at a higher plane and develop the pilot's view. However, to be able to do that, it is important to extricate oneself from the daily rush of activity and take the time and space to keep developing the bigger picture.
3. In conventional organizations, at the junior levels, the bulk of your learning comes from your boss. In start-ups, the source of getting better shifts from your boss to getting better by yourself. There are fewer existing answers, and so each time you get to an answer, you must practise review and reflection to get to the method of finding the answer and increase your core capabilities. Also, since many start-ups are

in the digital and technology space, there is a hell of a lot of online material available. An active process of leveraging that treasure and using the principles in Chapter 8 is thus important.

If you show the right work ethic, attitude to learn and willingness to stretch to make a difference, start-ups can be a tremendous place to build your long-term GBM in.

The professional's context

There is a large number of people—doctors, lawyers, architects and other such skilled professionals—who either operate by themselves or have a small group of people working with them. I like to think of them as a mini start-up. All of them start their careers with tremendous passion and enthusiasm. Some of them achieve huge success, some moderate success and some fail to make much progress in their careers. Again, I am convinced that the only variables that determines how successful professionals are, are their pace and breadth of getting better. There are two insights I have about professionals getting better, which I want to share.

Get better holistically—not just in your professional area

Success as a professional is not just about getting better in your narrow professional domain; it is about getting better holistically. Running a professional service is like running a business, and if you are an architect who is excellent at making creative designs for your buildings, but are poor at collecting money from your clients, you will soon fail. Getting better in a whole gamut of things at the same time is critical for professionals to succeed. Often, these are one-person armies and hence, there is even greater onus on that person to get better on multiple fronts at the same time.

For instance, if you are a doctor, clearly, an important area to continuously get better at is your medical skills—understanding the problems patients face, continuously evolving the treatment using the most modern and latest techniques and so on. But apart from that, you need to get better at handling the human side of the relationship with the patient. My doctor would often tell me, 'I have to treat your disease and I have to treat you, and these are two different things.' You have to get better at organizing yourself and your time. Imagine a doctor who is brilliant, but can't organize appointments properly and is inefficient with his time, which is his most constrained resource. You have to get better at financial management. You have to be good at people management, including managing nursing staff. And you have to get better at knowing where to locate your clinic, how to understand catchment areas, etc. In my interactions with many doctors, I have found that while medical skills are important, a lot of the difference in the success different doctors achieve is explained by how much better they have got in non-medical skills. The challenge is that the non-medical areas are self-taught, as the bulk of their education is in the medical aspect. Hence, applying the get-better principles of review and reflection to get better by yourself is important for professionals. As a doctor, your review and reflection cannot be only on medical aspects. You must review and reflect on whether your database for patients is organized, how it can be made better, how high your daily productivity is and what can be done to make that better, etc. You must get better by yourself in all the aspects that make you successful, even if many of those are not medical in nature. The doctor here is just an example—these principles apply to all kinds of professionals, be it lawyers, CAs or architects.

Apart from getting better by yourself, a vital aspect of professional success is making others better. Professionals often have a strong ecosystem—the people working with them, like the nursing staff for a doctor or a contractor for an architect. The ability of the professional to get the external ecosystem aligned to what they want to provide to their clients, continuously makes them better, and managing them effectively is a key area to get better at.

Disrupt yourself

I have observed in professionals that often, they settle into a pattern. A doctor might have a particular way of treating a certain disease and they tend to use that way for the majority of their patients. Architects and interior designers often become comfortable with a set of design principles and ideas and tend to use them across sites. For instance, an architect might favour using a high amount of glass in all their designs. Nothing wrong with this approach, provided that there is continuous validation that it is indeed the right solution for that situation and not a lazy application of past answers. If I were to analyse this using get-better principles, it is akin to the professional having arrived at an answer for a situation, an answer they feel comfortable with, and in the future, they keep applying the same answer for that kind of situation. It means that once they feel comfortable with an answer, they stop arriving at the answer using the primary principles. This is the beginning of stagnation of the get-better journey.

Having default answers also has a side effect—losing empathy with your client. When a client states a problem and the professional already knows the answer, they tend to short-circuit the conversation and go directly to the answer. They don't listen to the client empathetically because they already know the answer. It might be the hundredth time for the doctor solving that problem, but it is the first time for that patient, and if the patient feels that you got to the answer without listening to and understanding them fully, they are not satisfied. If, as a professional, you stop going to default answers and focus on finding the answer each time, it will not just aid your get-better journey, but also make you more empathetic towards your client. When you find that you are settling into a pattern of similar answers, it is the time to disrupt yourself.

Education and its impact on our GBM

One of the greatest applications of the get-better principles is in education. That is the only time in life where there is only one objective—getting better. We don't have to produce results for our companies or earn money or figure out how to rise in the corporate hierarchy when we are educating ourselves. In a way, in this phase, we do what I urge people in the working phase to do—we make getting better our priority. A lot of our ability to learn and the foundation of our GBM go back to our school/college days. Education has a significant impact on our GBMs. While it might be too late for many of us to change how we were educated, if we understand why our GBM is the way it is, we can take corrective action.

Let us examine one of the most prevalent techniques in Indian education, adopted by many of us in our student days—the rote method or the learning-by-memorizing method. This is the technique in which students memorize the answers to questions and regurgitate them in the exams in order to score well. Does this make you truly better? This method is akin to knowing the answer without mastering the method of finding the answer. While this might help you score in the exam, will this actually help you when you start a job where you have to find answers to unknown questions that are not from a question bank or past years' papers?

It works in exams because in many of our exams, there is a prescribed syllabus and the question cannot come from outside it. The questions are predictable if you work hard and examine the question papers of past exams. Hence, it is feasible to achieve high scores by the rote method of knowing the answers. However, in real life, in a job, there is no prescribed syllabus. Whatever be the situation you face at a given point, you have to find the answer to it. Also, in a real job, questions can't be predicted in advance.

In effect, our education system puts a premium on the answer and not on the method of finding the answer. Unfortunately, in real life and in a job, seldom can the answers you know be used directly. They almost always have to be derived from the first principles, which means you have to get better at the method of finding the answer. In one of the early chapters, I mentioned that the majority of the people I observed do not have a good GBM. One of my hypotheses for why that is is that during our years of education, we built a habit of knowing the answers and not the skill of finding the answers using the first principles. In many cases, that habit continued into our work life, seriously impacting the GBM quality. So while such people score in examinations, they might not score in the examination of success in real life and work. If you have, during your education, placed a premium on the rote or by-heart method, please recognize that *you haven't developed the habit of going to the method of finding the answers. You have to change your habit and build a new one if you want to build a great GBM.*

If you are still a student, focus on understanding the methods; don't focus on only knowing all the answers. Ask a lot of 'why' questions—when somebody tells you this is the answer to this question, ask yourself, why is this answer right, why not some other answer?

Equally, my suggestion to parents—and many of you are parents as well as teachers—is to let your children and students focus on the method of finding the answers themselves; build their skills and capabilities. Don't focus only on high scores in exams by feeding them the answers. The next time you are spending time teaching your kid, don't ask, 'What is the answer to 12 x 12?' Instead, ask, 'How will you find the answer to 12 x 12?'

In Chapter 2, I have given the golf example to illustrate how young kids have an extraordinary ability to learn rapidly. However, parents and the education system suppress that. Between the right answer and the ability to find the answer, we place a greater premium on the right answer. There are guides and books that give you the right answers, but for the exams of life and work, there are no guides available. What matters is the ability to find the answer, which unfortunately, we work very hard to suppress in the formative years of children. Liberate your children—don't give them the answer, but ask them to find it. If we all try collectively, we can change the ability of future generations to succeed, and perhaps the future of India and the world.

I do have a disclaimer here—I am not an educationist, but I do want to share my perspective to foment thinking in this area in each parent, each teacher, each student and in society as a whole.

Get-better summary

1. Getting better is not just applicable to conventional companies; it is applicable even more to the start-up ecosystem.

2. From a start-up company's view, their basic journey is about getting better in solving their chosen problem. If they don't get better rapidly, survival will be difficult. To get better:
   a. Founders and key personnel have to prioritize getting better and create the time and the space for that even in the frenetic environment of a start-up.
   b. Founders must move from an inwards mindset to an outwards mindset, which is more customer-oriented and not just technology-oriented.
3. For an employee in a start-up, it is mission critical to focus on getting better as employment stability in start-ups can be volatile.
   a. There is huge potential to grow in start-ups due to the absence of a well-developed middle management, and junior employees who show high initiative can use that space to solve more complex problems and get better faster. The space also allows for easier development of the pilot's view.
   b. Getting better by yourself is more important in start-ups. Online material can be goldmines as well.
4. For professionals, the difference between high success and low success is often how much better they get in their professional journey.
   a. Getting better for them has to be a holistic journey, not just concentrating on their professional area.
   b. They must disrupt themselves, not fall into a pattern of using the same answers again and again.

5. Education is the greatest get-better phase of our lives. However, by focusing on the rote/by-heart method of knowing the answers, and not on the method of finding the answers, we build the wrong habits, which impact our GBM in the future. If you are working today, you might have to recognize that there is this old habit in you and try and correct it. If you are a parent or a teacher, focus on building the GBM in the kids, the method of finding the answers, and don't place a premium on knowing the right answer.

SECTION 5

Most people suffer from the problem I highlighted in Chapter 8 on how to use books—the problem of assuming that because they have understood the content, they are changing and getting better. We established in that chapter that that is not true. You have to make active efforts to implement the contents of a book for it to positively impact you, and I want you to start that with this book. The next section will help you try and convert the principles and the content into an action plan.

When we think 'get better', there are two aspects we need to consider—the 'what' and the 'how'. The 'how' is the quality of the GBM, which is the pace and breadth at which you get better when you do anything, and the 'what' is the areas in which you need to get better.

We saw this diagram in Chapter 3.

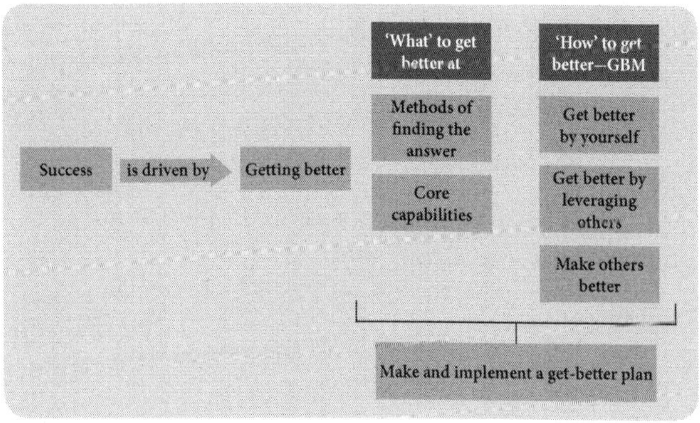

To get better you have to focus on the right 'what' areas in your context. The sum total of the areas we have to get better at is greater than our capacity to get better. Hence, we need to identify the most relevant areas for us in our given context and focus our attention on them.

The 'how' is about the quality of your GBM, which is the pace and breadth at which you get better in your chosen 'what' areas. That is based on how skilful and diligent you are in applying the 'how' techniques of getting better by yourself, getting better by leveraging others and making others better. The more you practise in a focused way, the better your skill in applying those techniques and the more powerful your GBM becomes.

In this section we will first self-evaluate how we have got better in our life till now. Are you somebody who has a great GBM and has got a lot better or are you somebody who has to improve your GBM and there is a long way to go? Knowing where we stand is important to making progress.

Post that, the chapter on making a get-better plan will help you identify the right 'what' areas for you to get better at and help build a 'how' action plan for that by showing a few samples.

Lastly, we will talk about creating the right enabling environment to accelerate the get-better journey.

15

Self-Evaluation

'That which is measured, improves.' I truly believe that to improve anything, we have to keep measuring it. If we act without measurement, it is unlikely to be effective. Let us assess that principle in the context of getting better—do we measure and evaluate how we have got better?

The only time our getting better is measured is when we are acquiring formal education. There is continuous and systematic evaluation of how much we have learnt, how much better we are getting. Of course, that evaluation happens through the school and the university system. Once we graduate and dive into our work lives, is there any evaluation of our 'getting better'? Do pause for a moment and reflect on the possible means of evaluating your get-better journey in your work life.

As we hit the work phase, the focus of measurement shifts from the measurement of our getting better to the measurement of the results we produce. Processes like business dashboards, KPIs and performance appraisals help measure how we are performing and the results we are producing. There is inadequate measurement of whether we are getting better.

Every now and then, there is some measurement of how we have got better through the career decisions our companies take on whether to promote us or not promote us, whether to give us the higher order job or not. It is, at best, an indirect measurement, and does not reflect accurately if we are indeed getting better, for the following reasons:

1. There is no transparency to that measurement, and hence, we do not own it.
2. It is a relative assessment, not an absolute assessment, of our getting better. Sometimes, we might not have got better at all, but because there are no other candidates, we get the job. It can happen the other way around too.

There is also a tendency to think that the results we deliver are an effective proxy for measuring our getting better. The argument in favour of it is that it is difficult to produce good results if you are not getting better, and similarly, if the results are poor, it does point to the fact that the individual does not have a good GBM. I agree with that in part—results are an indicator of getting better—but the assertion suffers several handicaps:

1. Our GBM is a part contributor to results, but it is not the only factor responsible for results. The quality of

our boss, our team, the external environment all make a difference to the results. Hence, good results do not mean a good GBM, and bad results do not necessarily point to a poor GBM. They are only an indicator.

2. Bad results can sometimes result in tremendous 'getting better' if the review and reflection principles are followed. Adversity is a great teacher. Some of the best phases of getting better in my life have been in the difficult-result phases. In this situation, my 'getting better' is actually moving in a direction opposite to my results.

In Chapter 2, we discussed how difficult it is to get better as we age. One of the biggest reasons for that is that as we age and get into the work phase, we stop measuring how much better we are getting. There are no external exams and we don't make up for that through a process of self-evaluation. And if we do not measure, we do not improve. Hence the first step is to get a sense of how effective you have been at getting better till now and how good your GBM is at this point of time.

There are five indicators to judge the quality of your 'getting better' till date and the cumulation of these five indicators will paint the picture of where you stand. These are explained below:

1. Self-awareness of our default tendency

This is a difficult but effective test of your GBM, which is to look for your default tendencies. Is your tendency wired to search for answers, or is your default tendency wired to search for the method of finding the answer?

Let us consider an educational example to understand this better. We have all attended these two kinds of exams:

a. In one kind of exam, we know many of the answers. We look at the question and then wonder which one of the answers we know fits this question.
b. The other kind of exam is where none of the questions have a direct answer. These questions require application of concepts. Here, when we see the question, we wonder which approach to take to solve this question, the method of finding the answer. Once we finalize the method and execute it, we arrive at the answer. In this situation, the answer is an outcome of the method we use. We do not look for the answer directly.

Similarly, as you face a situation at work, try and become cognizant of your immediate thoughts:

a. Is the first thought 'What is the answer to this situation?'

or

b. Is the first thought 'What should be the method by which I find the answer to this situation?'

If your immediate thoughts echo the second method, your GBM is robust. You will learn continuously and get better at a rapid pace. The more your default tendency is to look for the answer, the weaker your GBM is. Hence, assessing your first response and understanding your default tendency is a great way of evaluating the strength of your GBM.

Another way of thinking about this is to understand the difference between impulse and cognitive thinking. Impulse gives us answers; cognitive thinking is the method of finding the answer. What is your default tendency—do you go to the answer your impulse generates or do you practise cognitive thinking?

When I was the VP of sales and marketing at Onida, it was an operational job where many decisions had to be made daily and I was good at knowing the right answers to many difficult situations. Then I joined Cadbury as the head of strategy. As the strategy head, you have no control over which answers the business finally executes; that control lies with the functional and business heads. It was initially a very frustrating phase for me as I felt that my answers were not being given due importance. But then, I learnt that my role was to illuminate the method to the answer and not the answer itself, and that liberated me. But more than that, I think that role fundamentally changed my default tendency. Before that role, my default tendency was to go to the answers I knew, and I knew many answers. This role changed my default tendency and helped me sharpen the focus on the method of finding the answer.

If you find that your default tendency is tuned to finding the answer, rather than the method of finding the answer, it is a poor GBM and you must make efforts to change that. A few effective ways of doing that are:

a. Take on roles like the one described above, where the accountability for getting to the right answer is low and the focus is on the method of finding the answer, like consultancy roles.
b. Even in your current role, take opportunities to be a trainer or a facilitator. When you are a trainer, you are trying to help the audience understand the methods of finding the answers. You are trying to make them more capable, as opposed to being in business situations where you focus on providing them with the answer. Repeatedly exposing yourself to situations where you are a trainer or a facilitator can help you change your default tendency.

2. Pattern of the answers to your reflection

In Chapter 5, we covered reflection as a way of improving our capabilities. The question was 'why could I not get a better outcome in the first place?' and the answers to that question would be capability issues, which prevented you from getting that better outcome. Identifying the pattern of capability issues that surface in your reflections is a good way of assessing how good your GBM is.

If the same capability issues keep coming up repeatedly in your reflections over a substantial period, it is reflective of a poor GBM, an inability to get better by fixing those capability issues. Conversely, as you reflect over time and find that the capability issues that you discerned in the past have gone away, to be replaced by newer capability issues, it is reflective of a good GBM. In the Ajay-Sanjay example, for instance, Ajay's core capability issue was that he did not take the time in the beginning to generate a hypothesis, and rushed into action without thinking. If this issue comes up again and again in Ajay's reflections in the future, it is indicative of a poor GBM.

3. Leveraging external evaluations like appraisals and job interviews

Events like appraisals and interviews are great opportunities to assess our 'getting better'. These events happen infrequently, but when they occur, it is paramount to leverage them.

Appraisals often end up being an assessment of results. A good-quality manager would not only tell you what you did well and what you could have done better in the results space, but would also tell you why you did something well or why you did not do something well, i.e. their understanding of your underlying capabilities. If you have a good manager who goes down to the underlying capabilities, please make sure you note down what they say and work on it. Compare what they say with your own self-evaluation, the answers your reflection has been throwing up, and arrive at an overall list of things you need to improve on.

If you have a mediocre manager whose feedback stops at the results level, I urge you to do the following two things:

1. You can ask them follow-up questions on what they think is the underlying capability aspects for those

results, both good and bad. By asking the right questions, you might get good feedback.
2. You can reflect and pose questions to yourself based on the results feedback and arrive at the get-better list of capabilities.

Job interviews are another excellent way to get an evaluation. When a person interviews you for a job, they are effectively assessing the sum of your get-better journey thus far. In interviews, the questions are often about topics and situations you don't know about, and hence, test your ability to find the answer by the methods you have developed. We tend to focus primarily on the result of the interview, which is to get selected; we do not use interviews to evaluate our get-better effectiveness. You can leverage feedback from interviews in two ways to evaluate yourself:

1. Reflect on the questions you could not answer well. It means somebody expected you to answer that question well based on your resume, but you could not. Get to the why of that in your head. If you get to an interview and find many questions difficult, it is an indicator of a poor GBM and potentially low domain independence.
2. Obtain formal feedback from the interviewer if possible. Some companies and interviewers are open enough to provide feedback on the interview. At least in the cases where you get selected and join the company, you could definitely speak to the interviewer and obtain valuable feedback.

4. Domain change

Evaluating yourself each time you experience a domain change is the best way of assessing your get-better effectiveness. A domain change is when you change industries or functions or even geography, e.g., moving from handling the southern region to the western region. When you go through a domain change, it tests your GBM, because the answers you knew in the earlier domain are less relevant in the new domain.

If you struggle in a new domain, it is an indicator that you have a poor GBM, that your past success came primarily from knowing that domain well, not your underlying capabilities. And if you get to a new domain and fly, it is a great indicator that your underlying model is strong.

In my career, I have experienced both situations. When I moved from Asian Paints to GE Capital, I struggled to get going there. I did not know it then, but what that meant was that I had not developed domain independent capabilities in my stint at Asian Paints. At a later stage, when I moved to HR in Cadbury after having been in sales and marketing all my life, I found that I could succeed in HR, as if I had done HR all my life. One of the things that worked was that I took my underlying marketing capabilities and applied them to HR. I thought of the employee like the consumer, applied techniques of segmentation to arrive at different segments of employees with different needs, developed a positioning and a value proposition for each segment, and executed it. This is a perfect demonstration of how the method to finding an answer can travel across domains. Once you have a framework of how to approach a situation, how to solve a problem, that framework can serve you across domains.

5. Evaluating yourself by looking at your team

Evaluating the quality of your team, relative to the quality of other teams in the organization, is a great way of evaluating your GBM. I have observed that when a person has a high-quality team, they almost always tend to be people who have excellent GBMs themselves, and when people have poor-quality teams, their GBMs are the pits. This is often externalized and attributed to luck or to circumstances, but that is not the case. If you have a poor GBM, you are unlikely to be attracting high-quality people to your team.

These are the five different ways of evaluating, for yourself, how your get-better journey has been till date. I have summarized the indicators in the box below:

Indicator	Good GBM	Poor GBM
Default tendency	Looks for method of finding the answer; cognitive thinking dominates	Looks for answers; impulse dominates
Pattern of capability issues in reflection	Old issues go away and new ones surface	Same issues keep coming up again and again

Indicator	Good GBM	Poor GBM
Job interviews	Answers questions easily, even if they are about different domains or situations	Cannot answer questions about new domains or new situations
Effectiveness in a new domain	Easily effective without much teething trouble	Finds it very difficult to get going in a new domain
Team quality	High-quality team with high-GBM team members	Low-GBM team members, often experienced but not getting better rapidly

Do take a look and reflect and write down how good a GBM you think you have based on self-assessment of these indicators. Rate yourself on a scale of 0–5 with 0 being a poor, and 5 being an excellent GBM. A simple key to rate yourself is to see in how many of the five indicators you tick the good GBM box. If you tick two out of the five indicators, your GBM quality is equal to 2. Be honest in doing this: you are doing it for yourself, not for anybody else. Write down your GBM rating and the date on which you did this self-assessment below:

....

....

....

I want you to come back to this chapter once every three months for the next one year and redo your self-assessment. Each time you do the self-assessment, please do it afresh and do it with full focus and consciousness. Write down your assessment and the date in the space below each time:

....

....

....

Sometimes, people do get confused between the measurement of the GBM and the means of getting better. The above indicators are a measurement of your GBM quality, not the means to improving your GBM. To improve your GBM, you have to go back to the three components and practise them continuously and deliberately:

1. Get better by yourself
2. Get better leveraging others
3. Make others better

The purpose of evaluation is to improve by measuring. Hence, if you continuously evaluate your GBM, you will inevitably improve it. Sometimes, people find, through self-evaluation, that they have poor GBMs and get disheartened. Identifying the problem is the beginning of fixing it, and knowing that you have a poor GBM will set you on the path to improving it. If you find that you rate yourself particularly poorly on the GBM quality, it is even more important that you are relentless in your practice of the three components of getting better. There are no shortcuts to success, and if you have a poor GBM, you have to show the determination to improve it.

Self-awareness of where you stand now is the single greatest enabler of an effective get-better journey.

Get-better summary

1. What is measured improves. That is true for our get-better journey also. Unfortunately, we do not effectively measure getting better at work. We have measurement tools for the results we produce, but not for how much better we got producing those results and the quality of our GBM.
2. The five indicators for assessing the GBM quality by yourself are:
    a. Assess if your *default tendency* is to go to the answer, or to go to the method of finding the answer.
    b. Identify the *pattern of capability issues* being thrown up by your reflections and see if the issues remain constant for a long time, which means you are not getting better.
    c. Leveraging external evaluations like *appraisals and interviews*. Do not focus only on the results they produce, but also on the get-better feedback you get.

d. When you *change domains*, see if you struggle or fly in the new domain. That is the best indicator of your current GBM quality.
e. If you attract *high-quality teams,* you have a good GBM, and vice versa.

3. Rate yourself on a scale of 0–5 on the indicators. Reassess yourself every three months till you reach 5.
4. If you have a poor GBM, you can fix it only if you know about it and are honest about it. Show the determination to change your GBM if it is poor. It can be done.

16

Making a Get-Better Plan

I used to run as a hobby about a decade ago, and even ran a few half-marathons. After my first half-marathon, completed in 2 hours and 50 minutes, I was very keen to improve my timing and worked very hard for the second half-marathon. I practised for over two months and made a serious effort, yet the improvement was moderate. I managed only 2 hours and 42 minutes. The third year, I did not work that hard and put in a lot of hours, but worked on improving my running technique, specifically on lengthening my stride, so that it took fewer steps to complete the run. The result was magical—my timing came down to 2 hours and 15 minutes. In the second year, I concentrated just on making more effort but the gain was marginal. In the third year, however, I focused on getting better at running and for no additional effort, got much better results.

The key was the recognition that just running more did not improve my running technique; I had to work specifically on improving the technique. Always remember:

Success = Effort x Getting Better

The wonderful thing about improving my running technique was that not only did it enhance my results in the third year, it helped me boost my performance in every subsequent run I did. The same thing applies to work. Sometimes, working harder can get you better results, but that won't help improve future results. When you get better, however, it improves not only your current results but also your future results. The next time you get the urge to work harder to improve your results, pause and then redirect that effort towards getting better. That is what will make a sustainable difference. To be able to do that is important to make a get-better plan.

A get-better plan has three important steps:

1. Identify 'what' the key areas you want to get better at are. This should not be a laundry list but a small, focused list that is actionable.
2. Make a get-better plan, the 'how' to improve in those areas, based on the principles set out in this book.
3. Practise daily disciplined implementation of that plan.

Identifying the get-better areas, the 'what'

Making a plan starts with identifying areas you want to get better at. Ideally, you want to get better at those areas which will make the biggest difference to your current and future results given the context you are in. E.g., in cricket, both the batsman and the bowler must get better at running, but the context and situation for the two are different. Batsmen should become good at sprints to run fast between the wickets, while bowlers must become better at endurance running for bowling long spells.

The best way to find out what you need to get better at, given your context, is by disciplined practice of review and reflection for a while. As you apply review and reflection for a few weeks, you will start seeing a pattern of the areas you need to get better at. There will be some aspects that will come up repeatedly. Make a list of those—that is what you need to get better at. Significantly, it has come from your current context, from the most important things you do.

If it is challenging to practise review and reflection for every single thing you do, I recommend that you practise it on the important activities using the method below. On the x-axis is the amount of time you spend on a certain activity and on the y-axis is the importance of that activity.

Importance		
	Low amount of time High importance E.g., interviews for jobs	High amount of time Highly importance E.g., Customer calls, for a customer service person
	Low amount of time Low importance E.g., official entertainment	High amount of time Low importance E.g., paperwork

Time

I recommend that all the activities in the right-hand top quadrant be the starting point. Identify those activities and diligently apply review and reflection to filter out the areas you need to get better at. Next comes the top left quadrant—low amount of time but high importance. These typically include activities like annual strategy and budgeting processes, appraisals, interviews and hiring, etc. These are situations that don't occur often, but when they do, they result in important decisions and outcomes. Practising review and reflection on these activities should help you arrive at a list of things you have to get better at.

Let me give you an analogy to help understand this better. Let us take a street map of a large city. Just looking at the map, with the various streets and landmarks, one can get lost and not know what the next step is. To find the next step, it is necessary to know where you are at a given time, to locate yourself on the map. Most good maps also have a 'you are here' starting point, which provides clarity to plotting the next steps. If you don't have a starting point, you can't find a route to your destination. The review/reflection method for assessing your current get-better areas is similar. In a large map of many things to get better at, it helps you locate your current position and then plan the next step from there onwards. So please don't skip this step.

Once you make that list of get-better areas derived from your review and reflection, validate it by asking for feedback from your boss, your team and your family and friends. It is a very simple conversation; don't get too conscious doing it. Validating the list you made is important. You can use their responses to narrow your list to the top two areas; having a longer list usually does not lead to clear action.

Once you arrive at a final list of get-better areas, you have completed the first step of the get-better plan. Please do remember that this list is relevant only in your current context. If the context changes, for instance, if you get a new job, it is probable that the list will also change. So do refresh the list if your context changes.

Making the get-better plan, the 'how'

Armed with your list of areas to get better at, you arrive at the next step, which is to make the get-better plan for those areas. Some of the questions to ask to develop the plan for your identified areas are:

1. Which activities do I apply the review and reflection on to have the maximum impact?
2. How do I apply the pilot's view to those areas?
3. Leveraging others—which people do I leverage to get better at these areas?
4. Which books and training programmes will help me get a step jump in those areas?
5. Who in my ecosystem will have the maximum impact on those areas?

Let me give you a few examples to help you better understand how to make a plan. What I will do is first, identify the 'what' area for getting better at, and then give you an example of a 'how' plan that will help you get better in that area.

Sample 1: Get-better plan for hiring

A single mistake in hiring people for your team can be costly and impact your performance adversely. Hence, getting better at hiring is vital for sustained, long-term success. If your identified 'what' area is hiring, below is how I recommend you make the get-better plan:

The 'how' plan for getting better at hiring

1. Read the chapter on 'making your team better' a couple of times and understand the principles of hiring better.
2. Review all the past hiring you have done and classify it into good hires and bad hires.
3. Assess all the bad hires first and ask the questions:
    a. Review: What could I have done for a better outcome in that hiring situation?
    b. Reflection: Why could I not get that better outcome in the first place?
4. Then assess the good hires and ask the questions:
    a. Review: What did I do to get a better outcome in that hiring situation? What could I have done to have got an even better outcome?
    b. Reflection: Why did I get a good outcome in that hiring in the first place? Was it something I did or just good luck?

5. Based on the above, articulate to yourself your dos and don'ts for good hiring.
6. Prepare for the next hiring with those insights on how you will assess the candidate. Prepare the questions and the situations you are going to pose in advance.
7. Discuss your insights with the external ecosystem, the recruitment agency or the HR colleague, and make them better so they bring you higher quality candidates.
8. Execute this approach for the next three or four hires and then assess the results.

Sample 2: Get-better plan for prioritization

One of biggest 'what' areas we all could get better at is prioritization. We spend too much time and effort on trivial things and too little time on the important things. If prioritization is your get-better area, below is the plan I recommend:

The 'how' plan for getting better at prioritization

1. Make a list of the important things as per your understanding.
2. Refine that list based on the pilot's view—what is truly important, keeping in mind the big picture?
3. Validate that list with your boss.

4. Do daily review and reflection on where you spent your time each day.
   a. Review: How much time did I spend today on the important things as compared to the unimportant things? What could I have done to increase that time further?
   b. Reflection: Why am I unable to spend more time on the important things? Is it a lack of discipline, an inability to plan, an inability to execute a plan? What are my core abilities which prevent me, in the first place, from spending time on my priorities?
5. Identify books/training programmes on time management and prioritization and leverage those.
6. Keep doing the above till you see a material change in the amount of time you spend on important things.

I hope the above examples give you a sense of how to build a get-better plan. As I mentioned earlier, intent alone does not make you better; you need to have a plan. Once you have the 'what' and the 'how', the next step is disciplined implementation.

Disciplined implementation

Having a diet plan does not make you lose weight, implementing it does. It's the same for getting better—

having a plan is a great start, but the results come once you implement it.

The core issue is the lack of discipline to implement the plan rigorously. I have faced this problem myself repeatedly and it has been a challenging endeavour to find the discipline to do what is obviously good for me. I want to help you overcome that mountain, which stands between you and your goal, by sharing my learnings. There are three enablers to disciplined implementation:

1. Find a strong *reason/purpose* to implement the plan.
2. *Eliminate all excuses* and barriers to implementation.
3. Make a *public commitment*—make your plan public to be scrutinized by others.

1. *The reason/purpose*

We established in the initial chapters the following:

a. Results alone don't get you success. You have to get better while producing those results; you have to become capable of producing results in the future.
b. The responsibility of getting better lies firmly and squarely with you. Your organization and your boss might help, but the responsibility is yours alone.

Hence the simple reason 'why' for you to get better is your *long-term success*. If you choose not to show the discipline to get better and implement the plan, you are effectively making a choice not to succeed in the long term. Is that the choice you want to make? Like education, where the benefits are not immediately visible, if you don't find the discipline to educate yourself, your long-term success is compromised. Sometimes, there is no immediate benefit to getting better, but it is vital to long-term success. Every time you postpone implementing a get-better plan, remind yourself that that action is reducing your future success.

2. *Eliminate all excuses and barriers*

A good way to increase the probability that you execute the plan is to eliminate all the excuses and barriers in advance. Let me try and help you eliminate some of the common ones.

It is too difficult and takes too much time.

People often think that the effort to get better is too high and hence do not even try. I have two counterarguments to that:

a. We committed twenty years to education without any immediate benefits because we knew it was vital to long-term success. Why is it that after starting to work, we cannot commit one hour a day to getting better, especially when it has such a high impact on long-term success?
b. It is difficult only in the beginning—once you make it a habit, it becomes an easy part of your routine.

I will start implementing it from tomorrow/next week/next month.

Many people feel that while they want to get better, they are currently too busy to find the time for it. 'I will postpone it to the future, to when I am not so busy.' This excuse is used often, and it is important to eliminate it. Below are a few of my rebuttals:

a. Is a future where you will not be busy plausible? Is this a postponement strategy or just a lack of commitment?
b. What are you busy doing today? Producing more results? Is that result a guarantee that you will be successful after five years? Results have a finite life, often a year or two years. Getting better is permanent. Are you postponing a permanent gain for a temporary one?

It is beyond my capability to get better in that area.

Sometimes, what I hear from people is, 'I don't think I can get better in that area; it is beyond me'. This is similar to 'I always talk a lot; it is impossible for me to be good at listening', or 'I am too shy; I can't be confident in important situations, however hard I try'. Let us try and counter this excuse as well:

a. Are you correspondingly reducing your expectations of success as well? Or do you have a strategy of hope, that without getting better at what seems obviously necessary you will still succeed?

b. Getting better is a journey. If you don't start, the destination looks too far away, but if you start, each step makes it easier and brings the destination well within reach.

When you make a get-better plan, tell yourself, I am going to start this tomorrow. You will get much chatter back from your brain about why you can't. Identify that excuse and kill it. Kill every excuse every day, and then nothing can stop you from being successful.

3. *Make a public commitment*

Some years back, I started to exercise in order to be healthier. There would be occasions when I would have a late night, and so skip the next day's morning exercise. Then I started running with another person and I found that despite late nights and possible excuses, I seldom missed a session. The insight was simple—I had made a commitment to somebody else and I had to keep it. Sometimes, it is easy to escape the commitment we make to ourselves, but most of us try hard not to break a commitment made to somebody else. You can use this strategy in your get-better plan as well.

You can make your get-better intent public. You can inform your boss, your team, your family or your friends that there is a particular area you are trying to get better at and that they should observe, comment and push you in that direction. Even better would be to set up some kind of a periodic discussion with some of them on the progress you have made, and get them to share feedback. You will be surprised how much difference this will make in helping you implement your plan in a disciplined way.

Success is not about how good you are, but about how good a *model* you have to *improve* how good you are. That model is your ability to identify the 'get-better areas (the 'what'), make a plan (the 'how') and then implement it. And when you succeed in getting better at that area, you repeat the cycle for the next set of identified areas in a continuous journey of self-improvement. All the best; may the force be with you.

Get-better summary

1. Wanting to get better doesn't make you better; you have to have a get-better plan and implement it.
2. The first step of making the plan is to identify the key areas, the 'what' to get better at. This is best done by practising review and reflection for a few weeks and seeing what consistent pattern that throws up. Those are the areas you need to get better at, and it is good to shortlist two areas at a time.
3. The second step is to make a 'how' plan based on the key principles explained in this book. The plan must be specific and actionable.
4. The final step is disciplined implementation. To be able to do that:
   a. Find a strong reason 'why'.
   b. Eliminate all excuses and barriers in advance.
   c. Make a public commitment—be accountable to others.

17

Bringing It Together

Most of us want to be successful, and you are probably one of those, or you would not have reached the last chapter of this book. To achieve soaring success, we make great effort. Seldom have I come across someone who does not put in the hard work. We all hear stories of people working so hard that they missed their children's growing up years, or stories of people working day and night and on weekends to complete something important. There is no shortage of effort in our society. Yet, most people experience only moderate success.

Effort is the fuel of success. Getting better is the method to that success. Let us take an analogy. Assume you want to travel very far and you are willing to put in great effort to do so. If you put a lot of fuel/effort into a bullock cart, it is still high effort, but the distance you cover might be little. Instead, if you put a lot of fuel in a fast car, for that high 'effort', you will cover a great distance and indeed travel far. Unfortunately, most people still focus on more effort on the bullock cart and hence, never cover much distance, never achieve much success. If you do not focus on converting that bullock cart into a fast car, no matter how much fuel of effort you put into it, you will not be successful.

The bullock cart/fast car is a representation of your getting better. If you are getting better continuously, then, for the same fuel, you will get great success, and if you are not getting better, then for all the fuel of effort you put in, you will get limited success.

Never forget:

Success = Effort x Getting better

Attitude to getting better

One of the reasons people don't succeed is because at some stage of their career they get into a transactional job. A transactional job is a kind of job where it is felt that there is lower scope of creativity and value addition. In such jobs, it appears that there is limited opportunity to get better. Hence, one does not put in a focused effort on getting better. Then starts the downslide of careers—getting better is a habit and when you choose to break that habit for a period of time, it is difficult to return to it. It is important not to break the get-better habit and exhibit the right attitude of trying to get better in every job, however mundane and transactional it might be.

To start with, I want you to perform an exercise. Imagine that for two days, you are going to be the lift operator in a large office building with many floors. This is an extreme example of a highly transactional, executional job, with very little strategic or creative opportunity—or so most people would think. I want you to think about what and how you will get better at in these two days. Please take a few minutes and make a list before you resume reading.

I have done this exercise many times—the one big question people always ask is, how can you meaningfully get better while doing a lift operator's job? It is a very mechanical, repetitive job in which you ask 'Which floor?' to the person entering the lift and then hit the button for that floor. How can one get better doing that every minute for two days?

Before we discuss the lift-operator example, I want to give an example from my own life. This is a story I have quoted often, including in my previous book, *Catalyst*, but it bears repeating here. After my MBA from a pedigreed management institute, I joined Asian Paints. Early on in my training period, I was asked to man the godown as the godown supervisor had a medical situation. I drew a lot of sympathetic clicks and frowns from my fellow management trainees because I had been relegated to being a godown-keeper while they were learning and getting better at fancier stuff like sales and marketing. From their lens, the primary job of a godown keeper was to count boxes and reconcile the same with the incoming/outgoing document. A friend of mine, short-sightedly, joked, 'Since you are already very good at counting, there is not much you can get better at in these two months.'

I could also have approached it that way, and resigned myself to the fact that I couldn't hope to get much better in the months I was going to be a godown operator. However, I chose to go beyond counting boxes to identifying the get-better opportunities. Let me give you some examples. I could get better at understanding customer order patterns sitting in a godown: I could understand what the large city customers ordered and how that differed from what the small town customer ordered; I could understand the impact of promotions on orders—which promotions worked well, which did not; I could understand which items got ordered throughout the month and which items were ordered only at month-end. I could also see for which items the orders arrived in box loads and for which items the boxes had to be opened and individual items from inside shipped. I could also understand, while sitting there, that for some items, every box had to be opened, which meant the person who designed the box for that item had not done a good job.

As you can see, there were many opportunities for me to improve myself even as a godown-keeper. I did not stop at counting the boxes, but saw what else I could get better at and leveraged that opportunity. Let us now try and do the same for the lift operator and see which opportunities a lift operator has for getting better. Compare the opportunities listed below with your list and see what we have in common and also what you have that I don't.

1. Get better at understanding emergency procedures in a lift. What do you do when there is a problem? What do you do when you get stuck inside a lift and it stops between the floors? What do you do when you are outside and some passengers are stuck inside?

2. Get better at improving your memory and facial recognition skills. Try and remember which floor a particular person requested on the first day and on the second day; see if you can recognize the person and recall which floor they asked for.
3. Try and read moods and body language. Look at people and try and guess their mood—are they happy or worried? Read a book on body language and then practise it for two days in the lift. Study body language when people come in groups and based on the body language, try and guess if they are friends, colleagues but not close enough to be friends, whether one of them is the boss and whether that changes the body language of the group.
4. Try and study fashion. What are people wearing? What can you make of fashion trends standing there? Is there a difference in fashion based on age and which floor they go to? What if you were to write a report in two days on fashion trends to give to a garment company—what would you write in that?

For the purpose of being brief, I have not put down every single thing that one might do to get better even while being a lift operator. However, I hope you see now that the potential to get better is not determined by the situation or job you are in, but by your approach and attitude to that situation and that job. Even what appears to be a highly mechanical, repetitive job has get-better potential associated with it.

Once you bring the right attitude to the situation, the next step is understanding the get-better potential in advance. If you were to do a lift operator's job without assessing the get-better potential in advance, then, in all probability, you would end up performing a highly mechanical job and possibly not get much better. However, if you had done the advance listing of the get-better potential of that situation, like we tried to do above, then you would approach it much more consciously. I cannot emphasize enough how crucial it is to understand and determine the get-better potential of every job that you are set to perform *in advance*.

The right attitude is the starting point to the get-better journey. Getting better requires an attitude that I must learn in all situations and every situation has something to teach me.

The second significant barrier is the discipline to implement a get-better plan. I am stumped at how people are willing to work for forty years, 10–12 hours a day for success, but not willing to spend 5 per cent of that time in getting better to multiply their chance of success. How to find that discipline, that determination, is one of the most important puzzles to solve for you to get better. And a key driver is to create an enabling environment.

The enabling environment

We often use words like the 'learning environment' for schools and colleges. Sometimes, when people have to decide which school to put their kids in, they look for a good learning environment. The assumption is that the better the learning environment, the more conducive it is to their child's learning. A similar construct exists for getting better—the better the environment we create for getting better, the better the results. Except that the environment in this case is internal and resides within us. It is made up of our thoughts, our feelings, our calmness and our emotional maturity.

There are three aspects of the internal enabling environment that I want to discuss in the next few pages:

1. Setting a high standard.
2. Motivation for getting better.
3. Being a better human being.

Setting a high standard

All of us have an inbuilt get-better model. My tools and techniques will improve your model and accelerate your pace of getting better, and that is often the difference between great and moderate success. I myself did not know that there was something called a get-better model when I started my career and yet, I managed to achieve reasonable success.

A lot of what I have written in this book comes from experience—these are not insights I had right from day one. I did not know that one had to get better every hour by oneself; I did not know that I had to practise review/reflection/pilot's view. A lot of these I learnt over time and many of these, after at least a couple of decades of working. But that did not mean that my get-better journey started only after I learnt these techniques.

As I reflect on why I got better despite not knowing the techniques, I came to a very simple answer. My instinct was to always set high standards for myself—high standards of what I considered good, of the quality of output I produced. The high standards I set for myself often forced me to get better continuously to be able to meet them. If you set a high standard for yourself, there is no other way but to get better in order to meet it.

So apart from knowing the techniques taught in this book for getting better, I strongly recommend that you start setting higher standards for yourself, higher than those you have been setting so far. One of the big reasons why people don't get better is because even when they produce moderate quality output, they think they have done well. They have low standards. The difference between Sachin Tendulkar and many other cricketers was always the standard Sachin set for himself. His expectations from himself were possibly higher than what other cricketers set for themselves.

To set a high internal standard, you have to start by first understanding where you are setting your current standard. The challenge is all of us, all the time, think we are setting high standards for ourselves. We don't have any way of knowing if we are setting moderate or low standards for ourselves. A simple way of knowing your standard is when you do something that, in your own judgement, is good. See how many others spontaneously tell you that it was good. If you think you did something good, but not many people come up spontaneously to say it was good, then maybe you are setting the bar too low. On the contrary, if you did something you think was poor or average, and a lot of people come up and say it was good, then you are setting your standards high.

Let us attempt an exercise. Take a few minutes to reflect on the activities you thought you did well in the last three months, and then assess how many people spontaneously told you they were good. Then take a few minutes and list the situations in the last three months where you thought you did a poor or average job, and see if anybody said it was good. Based on that, rate your current standard-setting as low, medium, high or very high. Here is the scale I recommend for the rating:

1. Low: You thought you did well but you got some feedback from others that it was moderate or poor.
2. Medium: You thought you did well and you got neither positive nor negative feedback spontaneously.
3. High: You thought you did well and you got feedback spontaneously, without asking, that it was good.
4. Very high: You thought you did poorly, and yet you got feedback from others that it was good.

In the next three months, set a target of raising your standard-setting by one level, and then repeat the assessment exercise. Do this every three months till you reach 'very high', and then stay there.

Motivation to get better

Getting better is a challenging journey. A lot of people have the intention to get better, but lack the discipline and the focus to convert that intention into sustained action. Part of the reason could be the lack of powerful motivation to get better. Most people have the base motivation 'I want to be successful', often expressed as 'I want the next promotion, next title, etc.' While it looks like a powerful motivator on paper, in reality, it is more a wish than an impetus. It lacks the power to create the discipline and the focus that a truly powerful motivation can create.

To give an analogy, if any sportsperson, say Virat Kohli, has a motivation to be successful as a sportsperson, how motivated would they be to continuously get better? Alternately, if his motivation is 'I want to win the World Cup for India', my guess is that motivation is more powerful in pushing him to relentlessly get better. The movement from 'I want to be successful' to 'I want to win the World Cup for India' is a movement of creating impact beyond yourself. That is my insight—when your motivation has a purpose, has a cause for creating impact beyond just making you successful, it is a lot more powerful to push yourself to get better.

In my life, there have been phases where I have had absolutely powerful motivations and coincidentally, those were the best phases of getting better and growing. When I was in Onida, the situation I had mentioned earlier was one of intense competition due to the entry of LG and Samsung into the Indian market. There was a lot at stake for Onida. A large company like BPL could not cope and survive in that competition. In that phase, my motivation was often 'More than a few thousand people who work in this company depend on my performance for this company to do well. I must get better every day to sustain this organization and the people who work here.' That was very powerful motivation for me and it pushed me very hard to continuously be at my best and get better.

Similarly, in my first eight years at Cadbury/Mondelez, I believed, 'I am an architect in creating one of the best businesses and the best organizations that ever existed in this country, in this world.' That was a super powerful motivation, one that pushed me to continuously raise the standard of what was good for myself, and I got better continuously in that phase. But in the same company, towards the end, when the context changed from 'building one of the best businesses' to 'delivering for this quarter', I found that my motivation was not powerful. In that changed context, I could not find the motivation to get better continuously and it resulted in me stagnating in my personal growth. In hindsight, as I reflect, I do realize that as the context changed, I should have found a new way of motivating myself, but failed to do so.

You would have deduced from the sportsperson analogy and my own life story that having a powerful motivation is crucial to creating the internal environment for getting better. Ask yourself what your current motivation is, and write it down:

....

....

....

Getting better requires discipline and commitment. Ask yourself, will this motivation be powerful enough for you to create that discipline and commitment? Assess that. Then ask yourself, if I were to find a more powerful motivation, a motivation based on the insight of creating impact beyond myself, a motivation where I have to make a difference, what would that look like? Spend some time thinking about that and write it down here:

....

....

....

In my experience, failure is a powerful motivator. If it looks like you are going to fail, it's often possible to find a powerful motivation in the short term to reverse that. But it might not be sustainable. Moderate success is the worst place to be in, because it does not have desperation from the negative push of failure and by itself, lacks the power to motivate for a significant personal change. It is in this phase that you must find a more powerful motivation. Find that powerful motivation and you will be surprised how much your get-better journey accelerates.

Being a better human being

Many of the techniques I have described require us to be a better human being. Tools like reflection and pilot's view require us to be very objective and calm, and to be able to face truths without hiding from them. Tools like getting better by leveraging others and books, etc. require a degree of realization that we don't know everything, and can learn from others. Tools like making others better require a degree of selflessness. The ability to implement a get-better plan requires intense focus, discipline and commitment. Each of these is the trait of a good human being. The single biggest enabling environment you can create for getting better is to get on the quest of being a better human being.

Without claiming to be even a novice in brain science, here is my simple understanding of the relevant aspects. The brain has two areas—the amygdala and the neocortex. The amygdala is the emotional centre of the brain, and the neocortex, the more purposeful part, the thinking part of the brain. An overactive amygdala can prevent the neocortex from functioning effectively. We have all seen the people who get quite emotional, stressed out and easily distracted—signs of an overactive amygdala. It is difficult for such people to get better and their emotions often come in the way of their career success.

To create an enabling environment for getting better, for the neocortex to be liberated, it is important to centre yourself as a human being. I strongly recommend activities like meditation, yoga, sports, exercise, etc. as a part of your daily routine. These activities, apart from having several health benefits, have the singular effect of calming the amygdala and allowing the neocortex to enable you to get better. The more you practise these activities, the better your review, reflection and pilot's view will become. You will find yourself much more focused and disciplined in your get-better journey.

To be able to leverage others to get better and to make others better requires a degree of humility, an openness to be influenced and a spirit of generosity and selflessness. My sense is that a combination of spirituality and a culture of giving, i.e. a social or charitable commitment, create these values in you. By spirituality, I don't mean religion, although being religious can sometimes be a great means to being spiritual. I shall leave it to you to discover your own means to spirituality, but do remember that it is a great enabler to your getting better, apart from being a fruitful and fulfilling journey in itself.

Giving to society, making a difference to the world and charity are great human values. And as you start to give and make a difference, you will be amazed at what it starts to do to you as a person. In my experience, this benefit is achieved only when you go past writing a cheque once in a while to actively committing to contributing to society in some way.

While I have been writing cheques for many decades, it did not make me a better human being. However, about a decade ago, a truly immersive experience of contributing to society happened, when, as a part of Cadbury's CSR project, I was nominated to be on the advisory board for the project with the Sri Aurobindo Society in Pondicherry,

India. It was a transformational experience for me, and changed me as a human being. I realized that when you try to give, and try to give in a meaningful way, nature returns the effort manifold. You give time and money and nature gives you back a better human being. And better human beings are more effective at getting better faster and continuously. So give, give with a spirit of generosity, and give not just money but a part of yourself.

In our younger years, we have often looked with awe at successful people and wished one day to be like that. There are two kinds of successful people—those who are very successful and those who are role models to you. Not all successful people would fit the bill of a role model. I noticed that the crucial difference between those whose success was inspiring, and a subset from among them who became role models for me, was how good they were as human beings.

In my younger years, I often used to look at my role models and marvel at their multifaceted approach to work and life. It appeared to me that most successful people were not just slaves of success, but those who had interests beyond work, seemed very aware of the world and were seeking to make a difference. And I used to think, 'Wow, once I become successful, I will also then have the time to be multifaceted, with many interests and hobbies, and I will also make a difference to the world, but first, let me become successful.' It is only now I realize that it is the other way around. Those people did not become successful and then start being multifaceted and better human beings; they became successful *because* they were good human beings and multifaceted.

The greatest enabler to being successful, to getting better, is to become a better human version of yourself.

Success is the answer; getting better is the method of finding the answer. Success is the destination; getting better is the journey to that destination. And the fantastic thing about getting better is that it not only makes you successful, it also has the wonderful side effect of making you a better human being.

All the best for the journey of getting better and becoming the best human being you can become.

Acknowledgements

Getting better is a lifelong journey and I want to thank the many people and the companies who have helped me in this journey in life.

I want to start with my parents—my dad, in particular, who passed on his mathematical and scientific skills to me. My teachers at school and college for their selflessness in teaching me all that they knew without taking any credit themselves. And my fellow students, particularly at XLRI, from whom I learnt a lot.

My first company was Asian Paints, an institution made for making its employees get better. Every manager there takes the responsibility of training and developing the next generation and I was fortunate to be trained by some fantastic leaders there. My special gratitude to Amit Syngle—my mentor when I was a trainee and then a lifelong friend; P.M. Murty—one of the great business leaders of the modern era and an architect of the modern Asian Paints; K.B.S. Anand—a leader who is very simple and uncomplicated in his thinking; and P.G. Ponnapa—my boss for a few years who believed that bosses must be friends first. Apart from these leaders I was fortunate to have interacted with other senior leaders like Ashwinbhai Choksi, Ashwinbhai Dani, Abhaybhai Vakil, Jalaj Dani and Manish Choksi who helped me in my get-better journey at Asian Paints.

My stint at Onida was a fantastic get-better journey for me. It was a challenging assignment that stretched me significantly, so much so that I believe I learnt eight years' worth in the four years I spent there. Gulu Mirchandani, Vijay Masukhani, Sundar and Sasha were great guides in this phase. I learnt and got better from the passion and belief of every colleague and team member of mine who kept fighting a very tough battle in the marketplace every day with all their might.

Then was Cadbury/Mondelez—the place where I got better thanks to the significant variety of opportunities I got. I am thankful to the company for allowing me to move from strategy to HR to marketing to general management as well as providing the international exposure that enabled me to get better at multiple domains. People who actively guided and mentored me in this were Rajiv Wahi—a gentleman leader, if there is such a phrase, and Tim Cofer—the driven leader who led with his head and his heart. I also learnt a lot from my colleagues and peers there—Sanjay Purohit, Sunil Sethi, Sunil Taldar, Jaiboy Philips, Girish Bhat, Radhakrishnan Menon and Atul Bhatia, to name a few. Every team member of mine in this phase is special and some of them taught me more than

I taught them—Sid, Rajesh, Nikhila, Keith, Anil, Chella, Giri, Nitin, Amar, Arul, Indro, Sameer, Vivek, Savitha, Anupam and Shantanu, to name a few. I also learnt here that when people in the company are passionate and selfless, when every member of your team is passionate and selfless, it rubs off on you also. Thanks to every one of them for inspiring me.

In my few years at Pidilite, I have been getting better at learning organization transformation through continuous improvement and with the help of passionate talent. My special thanks to Pidilite and its leadership comprising M.B. Parekh and Bharat Puri for encouraging me to pursue my passion for writing books along with the job; not many companies are flexible and large-hearted like that. I am truly thankful to the company and my colleagues here for enabling me to use all the pillars of getting better—getting better my myself, getting better leveraging others and making others better.

I want to thank my publishers, Penguin Random House India, for their tireless work in making my first book, *Catalyst*, a great success. I especially want to thank Vijesh, Preeti, Sameer, Harish, Dada, Raghu, Sunil, Priyanka, Neha, Peter, Aditi and their teams for their passionate effort behind *Catalyst*. That gave me the confidence to attempt my second book. I want to thank Gaurav Shrinagesh for always making me feel special as an author and my superb editor Radhika Marwah, without whose effort this book would not be half as good and who is a wonderful partner to have in my journey of getting better as an author. Thank you, PRH. Let us keep rocking.

I want to thank the many people who read the book and gave me helpful suggestions on how to improve it—Bharat, Anand, Ponnapa, Garima, Chella, Nitin, Mandar, Sunil, Balaji and my dad. It takes a lot of time and active commitment to review a book multiple times and give feedback and I am truly grateful for that.

Shout out to the core group of dear friends who helped me market and popularize *Catalyst* and who have now embarked on the journey of making this book a success. They help me selflessly because they are friends and god bless them for that.

I also want to thank the many readers of *Catalyst* who messaged me on various social media forums asking me to write a second book, thereby inspiring me to do so. It is the love, affection and the encouragement of my readers that has made this possible. Thank you to each one of you from the bottom of my heart. I look forward to your continued support.

Lastly, my two gurus—Bharat Puri and Anand Kripalu—my mentors, bosses, guides and friends, without whose efforts in making me a better leader and a better human being, I won't be the person I am today. Thank you both.